BASIC COMPOSITION ACTIVITIES KIT

Bren T. Price

Bren T. Price has had more than 14 years of teaching experience as a classroom teacher and remedial reading and writing teacher at grade levels 4 through 12. He has also served as Director of Reading and Funded Programs and Acting Assistant Superintendent for Curriculum in the Phelps-Clifton Springs (New York) Schools, where he is currently employed.

Mr. Price has conducted a number of inservice workshops on "Reading and Writing in the Content Area" and "Instructional Guidelines and Activities for Basic Composition" and has also written instructional activities for curriculum objectives in the language arts and the social studies. He has completed graduate work at Syracuse University, the State University at Oswego, and the State University College at Brockport where he is presently working on a Certificate of Advanced Studies in Administration.

THE CENTER FOR APPLIED RESEARCH IN EDUCATION
West Nyack, New York 10994

Library of Congress Cataloging-in-Publication Data

Price, Bren T.
    Basic composition activities kit.
    ISBN 0-87628-169-2
    1. English language—Composition and
exercises—Handbooks, manuals, etc.
    I. Title.
    LB1631.P69   1982   82-12962
    808'.042

Printed in the United States of America

20 19 18 17 16 15 14

ISBN 0-87628-169-2

90000>

9 780876 281697

**THE CENTER FOR APPLIED RESEARCH
IN EDUCATION**
West Nyack, NY 10994
A Simon & Schuster Company

On the World Wide Web at http://www.phdirect.com

Prentice-Hall International (UK) Limited, *London*
Prentice-Hall of Australia Pty. Limited, *Sydney*
Prentice-Hall Canada Inc., *Toronto*
Prentice-Hall Hispanoamericana, S.A., *Mexico*
Prentice-Hall of India Private Limited, *New Delhi*
Prentice-Hall of Japan, Inc., *Tokyo*
Simon & Schuster Asia Pte. Ltd., *Singapore*
Editora Prentice-Hall do Brasil, Ltda., *Rio de Janeiro*

ABOUT THE BASIC COMPOSITION ACTIVITIES KIT

The *Basic Composition Activities Kit* gives secondary English teachers, special reading or writing teachers, and other educators concerned with writing improvement a practical, systematic approach to teaching basic composition skills. Easily used in junior and senior high school classrooms developmentally or remedially, it concentrates on four essential areas of composition and is conveniently organized into the following sections:

    I. Management Ideas and Activities
    II. Persuasive Writing Skills and Activities
    III. Descriptive Writing Skills and Activities
    IV. Report Writing Skills and Activities
    V. Letter Writing Skills and Activities

Section I provides practical guidelines and activities for managing the writing improvement program, including:

- an overview of the writing process

- prewriting activities to motivate students and to help eliminate the "I don't know what to say" and "I can't get started" syndromes

- modeling activities to develop students' ability to judge writing assignments and their understanding of the steps in the writing process

- conference and recordkeeping devices to guide students through the prewriting, drafting, and revision stages and to help them monitor their own progress

- activities and techniques for encouraging and building skills in revision

- evaluation procedures that provide for maximum student writing and require minimum teacher time

- techniques for helping reluctant writers

3

Sections II through V provide more than 130 reproducible student activities designed to teach students the basic elements of the composition process. The activities apply the common elements of standard English, such as mechanics and usage, to practical writing tasks. Each composition section also emphasizes key writing concepts such as purposes for writing, the intended audience, organizing ideas, and editing. If students' performance on state-mandated competency tests in writing is a concern, these activities will direct you toward their success.

Developed by a classroom teacher for classroom teachers, the *Kit* gives all teachers—even those with little background in writing or English—the information and materials necessary to teach writing effectively. It can be easily adapted to any content area in which writing is important. The additional components at the end of each section include lists of writing topics, model outline forms, and lists of signal words and phrases, along with sample responses to the student activities. The activities have been used in English classes, content area classes, and even Title I classes. They have proven effective in a variety of classroom settings and with a variety of students.

The *Basic Composition Activities Kit* offers a new and flexible approach to improving basic composition skills at the secondary level. It will enable you to revitalize and strengthen your writing program without changing your entire curriculum, and it will help you better meet the individual writing needs of all of your students.

Bren T. Price

TABLE OF CONTENTS

About the *Basic Composition Activities Kit* • 3

Contents

I

MANAGEMENT IDEAS AND ACTIVITIES

For many years educators believed that assigning topics and correcting papers on a regular basis was the key to improved student writing and successful writing programs. In the past decade, however, researchers have found that assigning and correcting alone do not ensure student improvement. On the contrary, the research shows that the real key to improved student writing lies in developing the whole process of writing. This process involves three essential stages—prewriting activity, writing activity, and revision activity—as represented in Figure I-1.

How can we, as teachers, find the time to develop and manage all stages of the process in our writing programs? Section I of the *Kit* presents a variety of practical management ideas and activities to teach the process of writing and thereby help students to become more effective writers. Included are prewriting activities, modeling activities, conference and recordkeeping techniques, student revision activities, evaluation procedures, and ideas for helping reluctant writers.

PREWRITING ACTIVITIES

Prewriting is an essential part of the total writing process, whether the writer is a first grader or a professional, whether the topic is student-directed or teacher-directed, or whether the genre is a business letter or a piece of narrative prose.

One important aspect of writing that should be emphasized during the prewriting period is *audience*. To whom are the students writing? Are they writing to their parents, the teacher, a close friend, or a prospective employer? The message may be the same, but the tone, style, and form may vary drastically. Make sure the students know the intended audience. Better yet, plan to have the students send the finished message to their intended audience. Writers tend to be more expressive and more precise when they realize the audience is involved.

The *purpose* for writing is another essential ingredient of prewriting activity. Is the student's purpose to describe, to inform, or to persuade? Is he or she writing a letter, a poem, or a report? Will the writing be published or merely kept in a folder in its rough draft form? How will the writing be evaluated, if at all? Is there more than one purpose involved? Students are not always aware that their writing is evaluated both on content and on mechanics.

All of the preceding questions need to be answered *before* students begin to write. Knowing the exact purpose and the intended audience gives the students direction and

FIGURE I-1
Structured Overview of the Writing Process

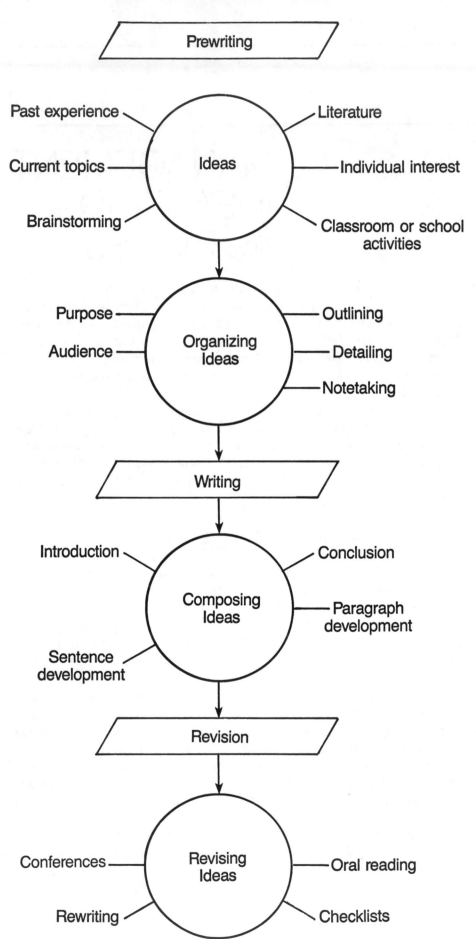

contributes to the overall quality of expression. The following activities should help to eliminate the "I can't think of anything to say" syndrome and get students started in the first stage of the writing process.

Teacher-Directed Activities

Here are several prewriting activities you can lead yourself:

1. Write a word on the board, such as "nuclear" or "subway." Have small groups of students list as many associated words as possible in four minutes. Transcribe these words on the board and have the students write sentences and/or a paragraph using the words.

2. Write ten vocabulary words from a piece of literature on the board. Have students write five to eight of them in a sentence or two. Share their responses.

3. Brainstorm or discuss with the whole class or in small groups: (a) pros and cons of a school activity or a controversial issue, (b) favorite movies or television programs, (c) an upcoming or completed field trip, (d) a photo, picture, or object, (e) a piece of literature read by the entire class, (f) a current event, (g) a classroom incident, (h) a character from politics, television, or movies.

The topics for writing are endless, and prewriting activity triggers ideas, words, and phrases to help students get started with their rough drafts. When the activities and topics are teacher-directed, make sure that all students have some prior experience with the material.

Student-Directed Activities

The following are prewriting activities your students can direct on their own:

1. Interview other people in the building (secretaries, teachers, custodians, and so on) and outside the school (firefighters, police officers, business persons, senior citizens). Write about them and include a picture with the report.

2. Using a simple questionnaire, interview others about their feelings, interests, and hobbies. Questions such as "What would you like to know about others?" and "What would you like others to know about you?" trigger ideas for student writing topics.

3. Brainstorm or discuss with a partner things that interest him or her. Keep a pencil and paper handy to record any ideas that occur.

Whatever approach is used, prewriting is important. Writers need this time and activity to think about their topics. Brainstorming, discussion, interviewing, and writing down key words and phrases all help to spark ideas they already have and help them put the ideas into print.

MODELING ACTIVITIES

Students may attend school for 12 years and college for four additional years and never see a teacher's writing product, much less *how* the teacher writes. Generally speaking, teachers assign a topic, collect the papers, and hand the papers back with the corrections. Most students note the grades and file the papers—permanently.

Do you know of a music teacher who does not play music or an art teacher who does not practice his or her craft? Can you imagine the outcome if these teachers never displayed their skills? Music teachers model position, movement, tone, and rhythm. Art teachers model form, movement, and detail. Both demonstrate in front of their students the process from beginning to finished product. At first their students imitate. Gradually the students begin to experiment as they practice and develop skills. Ultimately their own style emerges.

As teachers of writing, we must be aware of how much students can benefit from actually seeing our step-by-step process of writing. Where do we get our ideas? How do we organize them? How or why do we change words, phrases, and order? How do we write for different audiences and purposes? Students view writing as a one-step process, and we must show them otherwise.

Here are suggestions for modeling the writing process for your students:

1. **Prewriting:** Select a topic familiar to all students, such as "How I spent my summer vacation." Brainstorm on the overhead or board several ideas, images, words, or phrases that come to mind. Organize usable ideas.

2. **Drafting:** (You may wish to do this ahead of time.) Start writing in sentence or paragraph form. While writing, leave blank spaces if you can't think of an idea or word. If mistakes are present, let them be. If you are a naturally polished writer, make errors purposefully.

3. **Revising:** Display the rough draft. Circle words that may be misspelled, put parentheses around awkward phrases, underline unclear words, and cross out unnecessary ideas or words. Ask students to identify any problems you didn't notice and to offer suggestions for improvement.

4. Take the first five minutes of the period to write on the same topic assigned to students. Share your writing with the students and ask them questions about it. Be willing to accept suggestions if they genuinely help.

5. When teaching a particular skill, such as word choice, organization, or sentence structure, share with students a piece of your own writing that lacks the particular skill. Ask them to respond and criticize. Criticize your own writing out loud. Write a final draft incorporating changes and explain *why* you made the changes.

6. Use a form such as Figure I-2 on the overhead projector or the board. It is a model of an 8½″ × 11″ sheet of paper upon which you can use ⅔ to show your actual rough draft and ⅓ to include any comments or possible revisions of that rough draft.

FIGURE I-2
Model Rough Draft Sheet

(⅔ for your actual rough draft)	(⅓ for comments about rough draft)

Modeling serves a number of important purposes. It helps teachers as well as students appreciate the ease or difficulty of an assignment. It also shows students that there are certain steps involved in writing a quality piece. Most important, they learn that teachers are human and do not magically create and compose masterpieces on the first attempt. If we teachers of writing use the successful techniques practiced by our counterparts in art and music, students will see and hear models that they can imitate and with which they can experiment.

CONFERENCE AND RECORDKEEPING TECHNIQUES

Many teachers of writing have found the conference technique helpful in guiding writers through the prewriting, drafting, and revision stages of the writing process. The conference is used to let the author tell the teacher more about the piece of writing, as if the teacher were the learner. In turn, the teacher asks questions. The questions in themselves suggest a need for student revision, not teacher correction. The responsibility for improvement is thus placed in the hands of the student, where it belongs.

Questions for Conferences

1. Before we begin, will you tell me about your writing?

2. How do you feel about this piece of writing?

3. Would you like to share it with me by reading it out loud?

4. If I asked you to rate your piece of writing on a scale from one to five, with five being the very best you can do, how would you score yourself?

    a. If the student answers "five," then say, "May I offer one suggestion for improvement?"

    b. If the student rates the writing at less than five, then say, "What would you do to make it a five?" or "Fine, why not put it into your folder until later."

5. What part of your writing (beginning, ending, specific sentences or phrases) do you like best/least?

6. If you had all the time you needed, what would you do differently? (Have them write this down on their paper for future reference.)

7. What do you think a good writer does from start to finish? Did you do this? (This tells you what the student knows about the writing process.)

8. Is there anything that I can help you with on this piece of writing?

9. Now that we have had this conference, what will you do with your paper? (The student might respond that it will be handed in for formal evaluation, be revised and rewritten, or put in his or her writing folder for future work.)

FIGURE I-3
Student Composition Checklist

Name _____

Skill	Topic: Date Checked	Topic: Date Checked	Topic: Date Checked	Topic: Date Checked	Topic: Date Checked
Organizing Ideas					
Purpose					
Audience					
Organization					
Composing Ideas					
Introduction					
Topic Sentences					
Supporting Details					
Conclusion					
Revising Ideas					
Spelling					
Capitalization/Punctuation					
Grammar/Usage					
Sentence Length					
Sentence Variety					
Word Choice					
Sense					
Individual Checklist					
I read orally to					
Proofreader's Initials					
Date of Conference					

These questions help to draw more out of the writer. They also model the kinds of questions students could ask each other if they meet together in small groups. If you are critical or judgmental, students tend to be defensive and are afraid to open up. Moreover, your critical behavior will transfer to your students when they have conferences with each other.

Here are suggested guidelines for conferences:

- Limit the conference to five minutes.

- Give students an individualized checklist that includes things to do and skills to check before signing up for a conference. A sample checklist is shown in Figure I-3.

- Set up a conference environment that is comfortable.

- Provide a means for students to initiate the conference, such as the Teacher Composition Management Checklist shown in Figure I-4.

- Be nonjudgmental and patient.

- Listen more than you talk.

- Ask leading, specific questions that elicit expansion or improvement.

- Have students read the piece to you.

- Make a note of the student's strengths and weaknesses on the Teacher Composition Conference Checklist (Figure I-5).

- Have conferences in groups of three or four if possible.

Conferences are not easy. The class must be managed so that students know what to do while they are waiting. They could be having conferences with classmates, doing rough drafts, visiting learning or activity centers, brainstorming new topics, improving old topics, researching, or anything else related to writing.

Teachers who have successful conferences encourage student responsibility for topic selection, revision, and pride in the final product. These teachers tend to know quite a bit about students' interests, abilities, and weaknesses.

Recordkeeping

Keeping good records aids in the evaluation process. It provides the teacher with an up-to-date accounting of students' strengths and weaknesses, and it allows both students and their parents to keep track of progress.

The most popular means of keeping records is the use of a student folder. Students can make their own with construction paper, or teachers may distribute durable manila folders. In order to avoid a loss or damage of the folders, it is best to keep them in a central location, except during writing time.

FIGURE I-4
Teacher Composition Management Checklist

Name	Date	Notation or Activity	Rating	What's Next

Notations

D_1 = First Draft   OR = Oral Reading   + = Positive Rating

D_2 = Revised Draft   C = Conference   0 = Neutral Rating

FD = Final Draft   P = Published   − = Negative Rating

S = Shared with group

FIGURE I-5
Teacher Composition Conference Checklist

Name	Conference Date	Topic	Strength	Weakness*	Remedy

*Limit to one major weakness at a time.

Here are several suggestions for using student folders:

1. Keep a list of the titles of completed written pieces on the outside cover and note the date of completion.

2. List all potential topics for future writing on the inside cover. Also include here any special interests or abilities and areas of expertise.

3. Inside the folder keep any notes, rough drafts, and completed products—published or unpublished. From time to time these may need to be reorganized and rough drafts discarded.

4. Include a general checklist of skills discussed and any class writing ground rules. For example:

_____Write in pencil on every other line.

_____Do not throw away any paper.

_____Do not erase; cross out instead.

_____Do not go to the dictionary, teacher, or friend for spelling until you revise.

_____If you cannot think of the right word or phrase, leave a blank space and go back to it later.

_____Put your writing folder in the conference basket.

5. Include an individualized skills checklist in the folder. This should be very specific in nature. For example:

_____Placed comma between city and state.

_____Spelled "their," "there," and "they're" correctly.

_____Used quotation marks around speaker's words.

_____Tried to expand idea by answering "Where?" "Who?" "What?" "When?" "Why?" "How?"

_____Read what you have written aloud to yourself.

_____Read what you have written aloud to someone else.

_____Made any changes between the lines.

You may also wish to keep a separate classroom folder for diagnostic or anecdotal records on the whole class, on individual students, or both. These might include some of the following items:

- Writing samples from the beginning, middle, and end of the year.

- Anecdotal comments about individual activities, skills, strengths, and weaknesses.

- Classroom checklists such as those shown in Figures I-4 and I-5, with dates and times of writing activity followed by other desired information. (Figures I-6 and I-7 show examples of how to use the checklists.)

FIGURE I-6
Sample Teacher Composition Management Checklist

Name	Date	Notation or Activity	Rating	What's Next
Kathy	2/21	C	–	Discuss topic with partner.
Jim	2/24	S	0	Write second draft.
Barbara	2/27	P	+	Excellent. Select new topic.

FIGURE I-7
Sample Teacher Composition Conference Checklist

Name	Conference Date	Topic	Strength	Weakness	Remedy
Bill	11/10	Sports	comma in series	too/to/two	Individual instruction.
David	11/10	Books	using details	run-on sentences	Limit sentences to 15–18 words.
Jill	11/11	Pets	sentence structure	difficulty focusing on topic	Write 3 leads before writing.

STUDENT REVISION ACTIVITIES

Experienced writers know that revision is an essential—and perhaps the most difficult—part of the writing process. Student writers, however, may not revise at all because they view writing as a one-step process. How do we encourage students to write second, third, and more drafts so that they are genuinely satisfied with the product?

Researchers have discovered that a number of factors influence students' desire to revise.

- When students care about their audience's response, they tend to revise more effectively and frequently.

- Broad topics make it difficult to focus and organize. Students get discouraged because there is so much to say and, thus, have less desire to revise.

- If there is a specific purpose for writing and the outcome is tangible (publication, return letter, display, and so on), students take greater care in writing.

- When students select their own topics, they have control and a feeling of ownership. They will be more likely to change the material to be more exact and detailed.

- Students who write about personal experience rather than fiction or fantasy will be more inclined to revise for clarity and meaning.

- Peer audiences have an effect on students' revision and their use of new approaches to the writing process.

- Students need time to revise. If assignments are irregular and hasty, the pieces of writing will be disorganized and sloppy.

- There are several stages of development in revision, from none at all to complete rewriting. Students can be expected to advance and regress depending on topic, audience awareness, purpose, mood, and teacher reaction.

Here are some specific ideas for encouraging students to revise their writing:

1. Place an individualized Student Composition Checklist in each student's folder. Have the list checked by the student and initialed by a classmate prior to having a conference or writing the final draft. This checklist should be geared to the particular student's strengths and weaknesses. Gradually add new items as you learn more about the student.

2. Display composite classroom checklists covering general areas such as spelling, capitalization, punctuation, and mechanics. Discuss weak areas in small groups or with the entire class when applicable.

3. While conferring, suggest only one or two specific items to revise in the next writing or final draft. Add these items to the student's individual checklist.

4. If you correct papers, don't mark the whole paper. Write in the margin on the same line as the error, "one spelling error" or "word missing." Again, deal with only one or two specific items.

5. Allow students to use scrap paper or old dittoes for writing rough drafts.

6. Buy or make a rubber stamp with the words "Rough Draft" or "Under Construction." Stamp students' papers before they begin writing.

7. Have students write three different leads or introductions to the same topic *before* they begin actual writing. They can choose the best lead.

8. Encourage or require students to orally describe their topic before writing. This rehearsal in itself is a revision. For example, say: "Choose a topic about something

that has happened to you. Have a friend interview you about it. Don't start writing until the interview is complete."

9. Establish the following guidelines for students:
   - **Write on every other line in pencil and allow wide margins.** This automatically encourages additions, deletions, changes. Pen should be reserved for final drafts.
   - **Don't throw away any paper.** They can keep rough drafts to use as scrap paper. In some cases, words or phrases on earlier drafts may be picked up later.
   - **Don't go to the teacher, a dictionary, or another student for correct spellings.** Students will lose their train of thought in the interim. Ask students to write the word as they think it is spelled and circle any words about which they are unsure.
   - **If you can't think of an exact word or phrase, leave it blank.** Such words will be discovered during revisions.
   - **After writing your rough draft, put it away for awhile.** Time allows for thought, new ideas, better word choice, and more objective treatment.
   - **Don't erase. Use cross-outs, circles, or arrows.** Erasures are not any neater. If possible, give students pencils without erasers.

Teachers can play a significant role in encouraging student revision. Our role should be that of listener, moderator, questioner, and guide. Most people learn by doing, and students are no exception. The best way to encourage them to revise is to give them responsibility for it. Guide them—don't do it for them.

EVALUATION PROCEDURES

As teachers we may feel compelled to correct every error and every paper. This practice is discouraging because we just don't have the necessary time—especially if students write frequently. Moreover, students often react by ignoring corrections, disputing comments, or losing confidence in their ability. A returned paper that is butchered in red ink heightens their reactions. Consequently, this practice reinforces their belief that writing is a one-step process and that teachers have total responsibility for improving the students' work.

How can we save time? How can we place more responsibility on the students? First, we must assure students that not all pieces of writing are top quality. In fact, some will never amount to much. Second, we must help students to understand that rough drafts are not always ready for final evaluation by the teacher.

The challenges of time and student responsibility can be dealt with simultaneously using techniques such as the following:

- Make sure that students use the general and individual checklists before conferring with you and before handing in their final drafts.

- Ask questions on the paper, or preferably, in conference, that imply that revision is necessary.

- Use a system of peer evaluation in small groups or with partners. This will identify areas that require improvement.

You can also save time by using one or two different scoring systems to evaluate student writing.

- **Specific Skill Scoring** focuses on one or two specific skills per paper. The papers are graded according to students' ability to use a skill developed in class, such as the use of commas in a series, correct homonym spelling, or writing complete simple sentences. If this system is used its credibility should not be destroyed by evaluating additional skill areas.

- **Holistic Scoring** judges the whole piece, not its separate parts. This sytem gives equal attention to content, organization, clarity, usage, and mechanics. A quick judgment about its overall quality is made without redlining or correcting. If questions are raised by students, they are told the general areas of weakness and given suggestions on how to improve in these areas.

No matter what system of evaluation is used, the length of the assignment should be short and the breadth of the topic sufficiently narrow. A few sentences and/or paragraphs are just as effective as long, flowery passages or full-length term papers.

Grading for parents or permanent records is both necessary and valuable. Parents and administrators often ask, "How is Johnny doing?" A student folder with Johnny's writing samples, individualized checklists, first drafts, and final compositions speaks for itself. During the course of the year, pre-, mid-, and post-writing samples will tell everyone how the student has done.

Grading papers for a report card is obviously essential. Since every piece of writing does not represent one's best effort, why grade and average all of a student's writing products? Why not let the student select his or her four or five best writings for a grade for that marking period? Ask the students to choose their funniest, most informative, most convincing, or most descriptive piece for their final evaluation. This continues the process of self-evaluation and provides further incentive for improvement. In addition to the grade, the teacher might also report that Johnny has perfected two skills and will attempt to master several more during the next marking period.

"Why don't you correct everything?" some parents challenge. Teachers have two responses. One is that the paper may still be incomplete and in draft form. But, more important, we recognize that all people—students included—tend to learn one thing at a time. We work toward the steady improvement of specific skills. Moreover, correcting every error at once can be quite ego-shattering. Therefore it is good practice to encourage students to revise their own work to the best of their ability and let the teacher guide improvements one step at a time.

Another comment from parents is, "How can I help?" Here are five suggestions:

- Encourage your child to keep a private journal or diary. A birthday or holiday gift of a blank journal might be encouragement enough.

- Have your child discuss orally his or her topics for writing.

- Let your son or daughter read his or her writing to you—without correction or comment.

- Ask questions about the piece of writing similar to those asked in the writing conference.

- Don't write or correct for your child. Neither really helps his or her improvement.

Teachers must attempt to dispel the notion that we are somehow incompetent or negligent if we do not correct every error and all papers. If writers are to improve they must take part in the evaluation process. They must accept more responsibility for their own writing products and learn how to make improvements on their own to the best of their ability. The more teachers make revisions for students, the less the work belongs to the students and the less interest they have in it.

HELPING THE RELUCTANT WRITER

You may find the following suggestions useful in helping students who won't write or who have great difficulty in writing:

- Select meaningful topics. Let students choose their own topics whenever possible. Research shows that students who control their own topics write more and with greater clarity.

- Clarify the audience and the purpose. Make sure that students understand these before going further.

- Give students as many aids to writing as possible, for example word lists, signal words, and outline forms.

- Don't let students begin writing until they have jotted down notes or ideas and have organized them.

- Keep all assignments short. Long essays for reluctant writers serve no positive purpose.

- Show students how to answer questions such as "Where?" "When?" "How?" and "What kind of?" These help them expand their ideas.

- Give students patterns or models to follow. For example, "Mr. Jones, *who is the principal,* treats everyone fairly" models a nonrestrictive clause. Have students write several of these substituting for the italicized words.

- Write paragraphs with blanks in them, then write "what kind of?," "when?," "where?," and "how?" in the blanks. Have students respond to the questions in the blanks and rewrite the paragraph.

- Make sure that students use an individualized skills checklist geared to their strengths and weaknesses. Include "oral reading to someone else" on the checklist.

- Refuse to grade anything substandard.

- Let students select their best piece of writing for formal evaluation.

- Concentrate on *one* deficiency at a time. Correcting all errors for students will discourage them from writing more.

CONCLUSION

The key to improved student writing and effective writing programs lies in developing the whole process of writing, not just assigning topics and correcting papers on a regular basis. Prewriting activity triggers ideas. Modeling demonstrates how more experienced writers approach the task of writing. Conferences guide students through the whole process and attempt to encourage student responsibility. Revision by students—not the teacher—develops independence and self-improvement. A fair system of evaluation together with a consistent method of recordkeeping allows everyone, including the student, to follow skill development and overall progress.

By guiding students through the whole process of writing and by providing frequent opportunities for writing, you will see a vast improvement in your students' individual writing abilities and in your classroom writing program.

II

PERSUASIVE WRITING SKILLS AND ACTIVITIES

Although you may use the sections of this *Kit* in any order that suits your purposes, there are advantages to starting with "Persuasive Writing Skills and Activities." One advantage is that most students have opinions that they are quite willing to express, especially if the topic deals with issues that affect their lives. Many of the activities in this section are based on controversial and contemporary subjects.

Another advantage is that the concept of paragraphing is easily demonstrated in persuasive writing because students learn (or review) how to develop a single topic—their opinion. The section progresses from the single-paragraph model to a more advanced multi-paragraph format. The list of signal words and phrases on PW 41 also helps to develop the topic-subtopic-detail and sequence patterns of organization. This pattern development prepares students for the other types of writing covered in the *Kit*.

For the most effective results, teachers must guide students through the activities. Prewriting activities, such as brainstorming and group discussion, will help trigger individual thoughts. Teachers who write the assignment along with their students can either model the persuasive format or play the devil's advocate if the issue seems too one-sided. Using the persuasive writing outline form on PW 39 and the signal words and phrases can be especially helpful with less-able writers. However you can gradually eliminate the use of these crutches as the students gain confidence and develop their own style.

Persuasive writing and thinking skills will benefit all students, whether they are college-bound or not. The ability to sift through a mass of information and express one's opinion logically and convincingly is a valuable lifetime tool.

II. PERSUASIVE WRITING SKILLS AND ACTIVITIES

PARAGRAPH STRUCTURE

Information: A good paragraph is well-organized and discusses only one topic or idea. A good paragraph has three basic parts:

1. an introductory statement

2. a series of sentences to support the introductory statement

3. a concluding statement

Directions: Read the following paragraph and respond to the questions and directions that follow it.

There is no doubt that the Lions are the best football team in the league this year. In the first place, they have the most explosive offense in the league. Their average of 36 points per game proves this. Also, the Lions' defense is outstanding. It has allowed fewer yards per game rushing than any other team in the league and has given up only eight touchdowns in twelve games. Furthermore, when the score is close and the end is near, the Lions always deliver that clutch play to win the game. In conclusion, if the evidence presented above does not convince you that the Lions are the best in the league, then let their 12-0 record speak for itself.

1. What is this person's opinion? _____

2. How many reasons does the author give to support the opinion? _____

_____

3. How does the author prove that the Lions' defense is good? _____

_____

4. What is the introductory statement? _____

5. What is the concluding statement? _____

6. Which sentences support the introductory statement? _____

_____

_____

_____

_____

7. Is this opinion convincing? _____ Why? _____

_____

_____

ORGANIZING NOTES I

Situation: The principal of your school has given you an opportunity to express your opinion about changing the present lunch program to a "fast-food" operation. Check one of the following two choices:

1. I favor a "fast-food" lunch program. _____

2. I favor the present cafeteria program. _____

Directions: The following is a list of some ideas for and against the "fast-food" lunch program. Below the list, organize these notes into two columns. Feel free to add any ideas of your own that are not listed.

---

less expensive	tastes better
better service	no wasted food
more nutritious	better variety
wastes (more or less) paper products	
pays attention to students' likes and dislikes	

For Fast-Food Program	For Present Cafeteria Program

In the columns above, the ideas are listed in a random order that is hard to follow. Ideas must be organized into some order before writing. After they see their ideas organized, some people might even change their opinion. Did you change yours?

1. I favor a "fast-food" lunch program. _____

2. I favor the present cafeteria program. _____

Assignment: Using the notes you organized, write the final draft of your paragraph on the school lunch program.

ORGANIZING NOTES II

Directions: Read the situation and write the reasons *for* and *against* the issue.

Situation: In a recent questionnaire your U.S. Representative to Congress asked you to respond to the following question: "Should the military draft for both men and women over 18 years of age be enacted into law by the U.S. government?"

Reasons For	Reasons Against

Information: Writing out the reasons behind each side of an issue may help you:

1. Decide which side of an issue you support.

2. Express clearly your reasons for taking one side or the other.

3. Understand better what your opponent's arguments will be.

Assignment: Write the first draft of your position on this issue using the reasons you organized on the chart above.

AUDIENCE/PURPOSE I

Information: When writing a persuasive essay to convince someone else of your opinion, it is extremely important to remember to whom you are writing. Are you trying to convince your parents, a teacher, the principal, a board of education member, or a friend? That individual or group is your *audience*. Why are you writing to them? The reason for your writing is the *purpose*.

Directions: Listed below are three situations for which you may write a persuasive essay. After reading each situation, indicate the audience and purpose.

1. You have recently received your driver's license and would like to purchase a used car. Although there is enough money in your savings account, your parents are likely to say "no" to the request. Try to persuade them of your point of view. Give at least two reasons for your position with examples or details to support each reason.

Audience _____

Purpose _____

2. Because of an increase in burglaries and vandalism, the local city council is considering a weekday curfew of 9:30 p.m. for anyone under 18 years of age. The council has asked teenagers for their opinions on this issue before they make a decision. State your opinion on the curfew and give at least two reasons for your position with examples or details to support each reason.

Audience _____

Purpose _____

3. The new principal of your school has asked the students to identify the problems that exist in the building and to suggest how these problems might be corrected or improved. Describe to the principal two problems you have noticed in your school and give as many specific ways as you can think of to correct them.

Audience _____

Purpose _____

Assignment: Choose one of the three situations and write a well-organized, persuasive essay.

AUDIENCE/PURPOSE II

Information: The same message may be written in several different ways, depending on the *audience*. Are you writing to a friend, a teacher, a school board member, or a legislator? Your selection of words, your tone, and even your reasons could be drastically different when writing to these different audiences.

Directions: Read the two paragraphs and answer the questions that follow.

Paragraph A

I believe the proposal to change the legal driving age from sixteen to eighteen years of age in our state is impractical and would prove very costly to implement. First, there are currently 148 students in our school who are registered to drive cars to school. Multiplying that number by all the other schools in the state would mean that thousands of students would be required to seek alternative transportation. Is the state government prepared to pay the cost of all the new school buses that would be needed to transport these students? Second, many teenagers in this bracket have full- or part-time jobs and need to drive back and forth to work. Also, many families—especially those living in rural and suburban areas—rely on their older teenagers to help with necessary chores requiring transportation, such as shopping. In conclusion, sir, I urge you to reject this proposal because it is impractical and is likely to be very expensive to carry out.

Paragraph B

As the educational leaders in our community, I hope you are aware of the reasons why the proposal to change the legal driving age from sixteen to eighteen is unrealistic. Almost 150 students now drive to school in cars, and many of them participate in the work-study program you adopted two years ago. Very few of these students could continue in the program without their own means of transportation. Also consider the many students who participate in extracurricular activities like band, dramatics, and athletics. How would they get to and from school at odd hours? In addition, imagine what would happen if 150 more students decided to ride the buses to school tomorrow morning. I think you understand the problems that would be caused—especially to the taxpayers! For the reasons stated above, I urge you to contact our state legislator and encourage him to reject this proposal.

1. Who is the audience in Paragraph A? _____

   In Paragraph B? _____

2. What is the purpose of Paragraph A? _____

   Of Paragraph B? _____

Assignment: The editor of your local newspaper agrees with the proposal to raise the legal driving age. Write this person a persuasive paragraph trying to change his or her mind. You may want to use the same reasons given above, or examples different from those given in the paragraphs.

AUDIENCE/PURPOSE III

Situation: Because of declining enrollments and increased costs, there is a possibility that several boys' and girls' sports, including tennis, golf, and softball, will be dropped next year. In addition, courses in art and industrial arts may also be cut.

Directions: Select two of the audiences listed below and write a persuasive paragraph to each. In each paragraph give at least two reasons why you support or reject either of the cuts in the school program. Support your reasons with good examples or details. Try to write each paragraph differently, using a different tone, a different selection of words, and different reasons.

1. friend
2. principal
3. superintendent of schools
4. board of education member
5. parents
6. athletic director

Paragraph 1

Audience _____

Purpose _____

_____

_____

_____

_____

_____

_____

Paragraph 2

Audience _____

Purpose _____

_____

_____

_____

_____

_____

WRITING INTRODUCTIONS I

Information: You have learned that there are three basic parts to a well-written paragraph. For some people, it helps to use one of the phrases listed below when writing the paragraph's introductory statement. Can you add any others to the list?

From my point of view ...   I disagree that ...
In my opinion ...   I maintain that ...
It is my belief that ...   There is no doubt that ...
I question whether ...

Directions: Three topics are listed below. After thinking about each one, write an introductory statement for each. You may use any of the phrases above or any other phrases you can think of in writing the statements.

1. cheating _____

_____

_____

_____

2. physical fitness _____

_____

_____

_____

3. going steady _____

_____

_____

_____

_____

Assignment: Write a short paragraph on one of the topics. First organize your notes both *for* and *against* the topic. Then begin the paragraph by stating your opinion in the introductory statement. Complete the paragraph by giving at least two reasons to support your opinion.

WRITING INTRODUCTIONS II

Directions: Read the following situation, questions and sample answers, and sample introduction.

Situation: The junior class has $1,400 in its treasury. The class officers have invited you and all other members of the class to submit suggestions for using the money in your senior year. Each student has been asked to state what he or she would do with the money and to give at least two reasons why the idea is a good one.

Questions and Sample Answers

1. Who is the audience? *The class officers*

2. What is the purpose? *To suggest how the class will spend its money*

3. What is your opinion? *We should use the money to help pay for a senior class trip to Washington, D.C.*

4. What are your reasons? a. *educational*
                                b. *entertaining*
                                c. *memory not soon forgotten*

Sample Introduction

In my opinion, our class should use the $1,400 in our treasury to help finance a senior trip to Washington, D.C. during our spring vacation. Let me explain why I think this trip would be very educational, entertaining, and memorable.

Assignment: Reread the situation, then write your own answers to the questions and write your own introduction. Finally, complete the paragraph(s) explaining the reasons for your opinion.

SUPPORTING YOUR OPINION I

Information: Anybody can state an opinion, but not everyone is able to convince someone else with solid reasons or examples *why* his opinion is a good one.

After writing and_____?_____your notes, you should then write your_____?_____. After writing this opinion, support it with convincing reasons or examples.

It is often helpful to use one of the words or phrases in the box below to let the reader know exactly what and where your reasons are.

first	furthermore	equally important
in the first place	also	in addition
second	moreover	likewise
third, etc.	again	similarly
next	besides	finally
further	last	

Directions: Read the paragraph below. It does not use any of the linking phrases or words listed in the box. Answer the questions that follow the paragraph.

In my opinion, the school cafeteria should offer a salad bar as well as the hot lunch counter already available. The present hot lunches are very starchy and fattening. Some students would probably waste less food because they would only serve themselves what they really like. Salad lunches don't give you that slow, heavy feeling that makes it difficult to work in the afternoon. When students are served tray lunches they only eat what they like, so they probably don't get a very balanced meal. For the reasons above, you can understand why I feel a salad bar should be offered as part of our cafeteria menu.

How many reasons are given to support the opinion that a salad bar should be offered?_____Where do each of these

reasons begin?_____

Write the first two words of each sentence that is a reason supporting the opinion._____

_____

_____

_____

Assignment: Rewrite the paragraph using a linking phrase at the beginning of each sentence that gives a reason supporting the opinion.

SUPPORTING YOUR OPINION II

Information: It is sometimes hard to think of ideas that will help you support or reject an issue. If you could remember a few key words that relate to almost any issue, you might be able to get started.

Directions: Study the list of "trigger words" in the box below. Then read the situation and write an opinion statement. Choose three of the trigger words and write how you might use these words to support your opinion.

Trigger Words

money	safety	friendship	education	responsibility
time	energy	equality	environment	transportation
health	danger	pleasure	cooperation	conservation

Situation: Your friend, who attends college in a city 65 miles from your home, has invited you to attend Spring Weekend. Other than going away to camp for two weeks, you have never been away from home without your parents or other family members present. You are not sure how your parents will react. Therefore, you have decided to write for their permission to go.

1. Opinion statement _____

_____

2. Trigger word #1 _____How will this support your reason?

_____

_____

3. Trigger word #2 _____How will this support your reason?

_____

_____

4. Trigger word #3 _____How will this support your reason?

_____

_____

Assignment: Write the paragraph to your parents using the four points described above to support your opinion.

DEVELOPING YOUR REASONS I

Information: It is sometimes not convincing enough to just give a reason that supports your opinion. It may be necessary to go into detail about each reason so that the reader knows exactly what you mean.

Directions: Read the following paragraphs and decide which one is more convincing.

Paragraph A

Snowmobiles are dangerous to operate and destructive to property. First of all, many snowmobile drivers haven't had the necessary experience and some have not even learned the safety regulations. You can see why there were three deaths and over 35 accidents related to snowmobiles in our county last year. Snowmobiles can also destroy property. Last year the county sheriff received more than 20 complaints about damage to fruit tree orchards and wheat fields caused by snowmobiles. In addition, many fences were knocked down. As I have said, snowmobiles are both dangerous and destructive.

Paragraph B

Snowmobiles are dangerous to operate and destructive to property. First of all, many snowmobile drivers don't know how to operate them. They just buy them and then drive them. Second, many of these drivers have never learned the rules and regulations. Finally, snowmobiles damage property belonging to others. People who ride on them and damage property don't respect other people's property. To sum up, snowmobiles are dangerous to operate and destructive to other people's property.

Which paragraph is more convincing? _____ Why? _____

_____

_____

Sometimes you need more information about each reason in order to make your argument a stronger one. Try to think of any examples, facts, figures, or any other details that prove your reason.

Assignment: Select a topic from the choices below and write a paragraph about it. First you will write any _____ you can think of. Next you will _____ those notes. Then you will write your _____.

1. Teenagers are lazy   2. Homework is a waste of time

Remember: Use examples, details, and facts to support your reasons.

DEVELOPING YOUR REASONS II

Information: When developing a reason for your opinion, how many facts, examples, or details will you use to support it? If you expand the examples or details beyond three sentences, then it is best to present another reason in a separate paragraph.

How do you develop a reason? By asking certain questions (When? Where? Who? What? What happens? How? What kind of?) it is easy to expand the reason.

Directions: Read part of the opinion statement and the questions and paragraph that follow.

"Snowmobiles are dangerous to operate"

When? when people are inexperienced; when conditions are poor
Where? in unfamiliar areas; away from marked trails
Who or What? those who haven't learned safety rules
What kind of? foolish; poorly maintained snowmobiles
Why? because some are careless or don't think; some drive too fast
What happens? accidents; injuries; deaths

Snowmobiles are dangerous to operate. This is especially true when they are driven by inexperienced or untrained people who have not learned the safety regulations. They are also dangerous when weather conditions are poor and when people drive them off trails or in areas with which they are unfamiliar. It is a known fact that many accidents occur because operators drive too fast or owners do not properly maintain their vehicles. You can understand, therefore, why there were three deaths and more than 35 accidents related to snowmobiles in our county last year.

Assignment: You have just read an example of how an opinion statement can be expanded into a paragraph by answering several basic questions. Read the following opinion statement and write answers to the same questions. Then write those answers in paragraph form.

"Snowmobiles are destructive to property."

When? _____

Where? _____

Who or What? _____

What kind of? _____

Why? _____

What happens? _____

WRITING CONCLUSIONS I

Information: It has been said that every successful movie has a powerful ending. A strong paragraph also has a powerful ending, or *conclusion*. At first, your conclusion might just be a repetition of the introduction. As you improve in your writing, however, your conclusion may summarize the whole paragraph. You might even offer some kind of solution in the conclusion.

Just as some people like to use an introductory phrase before their introduction, others like to use a concluding phrase before their conclusion. Look at the list of these words or phrases in the box below. Be sure to use a comma after any of the concluding phrases listed.

for the reasons given above	in summation
for the preceding reasons	in conclusion
as you can see	in other words
in sum	as I have noted above
to sum up	without a doubt
in brief	in any case
on the whole	in the final analysis
in short	in any event

Directions: Read the paragraph below and write a conclusion for it. Use a concluding phrase to get started if you need it. Compare yours with those of others in the class.

The most exciting form of entertainment for me is watching a horse race at a racetrack. My excitement starts to build while I watch the horses warm up before each race. It mounts as the horses approach the starting gate and the crowd hushes, directing its attention to the starting bell. As the race begins, I am almost bursting with the thrill of the competition. My eyes are glued to the horses as they round the track for the final stretch. I feel a shout of joy or a groan of disappointment escaping me as the horses cross the finish line.

_____

_____

_____

_____

WRITING CONCLUSIONS II

Information: You know that a conclusion can be merely a restatement of the introduction. Sometimes, however, it is necessary to expand that restatement into a separate paragraph. How do you expand a conclusion? Read the questions and answers below and notice how the questions have been answered in the sample conclusion.

1. Have you repeated your opinion? This is a must.

2. Did you use a signal word or phrase? It helps.

3. Who is your audience? It is polite to mention the name(s).

4. What are your reasons? Include the key words from each in your conclusion.

5. Can you offer another solution to the problem? Think of one.

Sample Conclusion

(2) <u>As you can see,</u> (3) <u>Mr. Silver,</u> your proposal to cancel our field trip to the United Nations and New York City (1) <u>is questionable.</u> If you did this, you would not only (4) <u>be punishing the whole class</u> for the foolish acts of a few, but also (4) <u>be denying an educational and cultural opportunity</u> of a lifetime to the majority of us responsible seniors. Why not consider an alternative solution, such as (5) <u>providing early transportation home</u> for those who misbehave?

Directions: Read the following situation. List your opinion, at least two reasons or examples for that opinion, and any details that support the reasons or examples. Finally, write a conclusion by answering as many of the five questions above as possible.

Situation: In your school there have been several thefts from lockers and empty classrooms during class periods. Mr. Howard, the assistant principal, has notified all teachers that students may no longer leave class or study hall during class periods, except for emergencies. Write to Mr. Howard expressing your opinion about his decision.

REVISING I: MECHANICS

Information: When you write the first draft of an essay, you are more interested in organizing your thoughts and information in sentences and paragraphs than in things such as spelling. It is only natural to make errors in spelling, capitalization, punctuation, and grammar. It is important to read through your rough drafts carefully looking for any errors. Many people also read them orally to see if they "sound" right.

Directions: Read the paragraph below and look for any mechanical errors.

I prefer to live in the Country rather than the City for several reasons. Their is less air pollution in the Country. Because there is fewer cars and factories to spew poisonous hydrocarbons into the air. Living in the Country better for you're health. Also, Country living is superior because of the extra available to grow fresh fruits, vegetables and flowers. Furthermore everyone know there is a lower crime rate in the city. Their will be less chance of someone hurting you. I guess you can understand why I prefer to live in the Country.

   Check any problem areas found in the paragraph.

_____spelling   _____punctuation

_____grammar   _____words omitted

_____capitalization   _____other

Assignment: By yourself or with a small group, revise and rewrite the paragraph to eliminate the mechanical errors.

REVISING II: EDITING

Information: Most writers are well aware of the need to make revisions in their rough drafts in the areas of spelling, punctuation, capitalization, and word usage. However, it is also important to check for other problems. Sometimes we put words or phrases in the wrong place, repeat ideas, forget to write an introduction or conclusion, include unrelated information, or even write in a disorganized way.

Directions: Read the paragraph below and look for any editorial errors.

Year-round school calendars should be adopted in our state beginning next year. When we close our schools for long periods of extended time, we are wasting space. When we waste space, we also at the same time waste money. My cousin goes to a year-round school in Florida, but he dislikes it. Why spend thousands of dollars on expensive buildings when we don't use them 75-80 days in the whole year? When we send students home for long vacations, they usually get bored after the first ten days anyway. Schools should be open year-round with short, ten-day vacations in between ten weeks of classes when it will be more better to operate next year when inflation soars even higher.

Check any problem areas found in the paragraph.

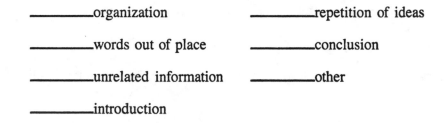

_____organization   _____repetition of ideas

_____words out of place   _____conclusion

_____unrelated information _____other

_____introduction

Assignment: Revise and rewrite the paragraph to eliminate the editorial errors.

REVISING III: WORD CHOICE

Information: When you write a first draft you are most interested in getting the ideas and information on paper. Therefore, you do not always think of the best word or phrase at that time. Sometimes you put a word or phrase in the wrong place. Other times you use a word or phrase too often. While reading through your first draft, you may decide to replace a word or phrase with a more precise word.

Directions: Read the paragraphs below and circle any words or phrases that are overused, cross out any unnecessary words, and underline any words that can be expressed more precisely.

Some people think "camping out" means going to an electrified campsite in their $10,000 travel trailers. They have all the comforts of home, including soft beds, bathrooms, and heaters or air conditioners. They have all the camping supplies to cook outdoors, but instead they have to go to the store to buy prepared foods to cook in the travel trailer. They even have refrigerators, stoves, and television sets.

I think camping means going to an outside area where you can pitch a tent and cook a meal on an open fire, without hearing a television or radio blaring. I think camping means walking to an area where animals roam free and talk to each other. I think it means sleeping on the ground in a tent. In conclusion, camping should be a getaway from home, not a home away from home.

The paragraphs above have many characteristics of an excellent essay. They are well-organized and have no errors in mechanics. However, repetition of words and poor word selection have weakened the message.

Assignment: Rewrite the paragraphs using more accurate and varied words.

WRITING SENTENCES I: COMBINING

Directions: Read the following paragraph.

There is more to do with your spare time in the city than in the country. You can go to a big-league game. You can sometimes visit a museum, a zoo, or a park. I like going to the movies. There are many movies from which you can choose in a big city. People live closer together there than they do in the country. There are more kids to do things with. It is easy to travel around for all these activities in the city. The public transportation is excellent. I really believe that the city offers much more to do with your spare time.

Check any problem areas found in the paragraph.

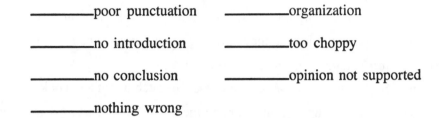

_____poor punctuation   _____organization

_____no introduction   _____too choppy

_____no conclusion   _____opinion not supported

_____nothing wrong

Information: There is a problem with the paragraph. Although there are no obvious mistakes, the paragraph reads choppily. All of the sentences are short, with a simple subject and a simple predicate. Why not try to combine some of the ideas into longer sentences? The paragraph will read better when you do.

Assignment: Use the connecting words in the box below to rewrite the paragraph. When you are done, compare your sentences with those of others in the class.

or	because
and	but
therefore	for
yet	so

WRITING SENTENCES II: MORE COMBINING

Information: You have learned that simple sentences can be combined into longer, more complicated sentences by using certain connecting words such as *but, or, for, and, so, therefore, nor,* and *yet*.
There are additional connecting words that you can use to combine simple sentences. These are listed in the box below.

though	before	when	as long as
if	as	while	whenever
as if	as soon as	because	due to
although	since	because of	even though
after	until	unless	in order to

Directions: These connecting words can be used in either the first part of the sentence or the last part of the sentence. Read the examples:

1. Jim had an accident. The party was over.
   Jim had an accident <u>after</u> the party was over.

   > OR

   <u>After</u> the party was over, Jim had an accident.

2. Her car did start. She decided to walk.
   <u>Even though</u> her car did start, she decided to walk.

   > OR

   She decided to walk <u>even though</u> her car did start.

Assignment: Using the connecting words listed above, combine the following sentences in two different ways, as shown above.

1. Frank will be the boss. John returns to work.

2. My vegetables were destroyed. We had temperatures below freezing.

3. I could not concentrate on the speech. People were whispering to each other all around me.

4. You set up the tent behind the barn. I will make sure the owner gives us permission.

WRITING SENTENCES III: FRAGMENTS AND RUN-ONS

Information: Two frequent errors in writing are sentence fragments and run-on sentences. What are they? Look at the examples below.

Fragments	**Sentences**
(Don't express complete thoughts)	(Do express complete thoughts)
1. When the boys left home.	1. When the boys left home, I was very lonely.
2. All the girls in the chorus.	2. I felt sorry for all the girls in the chorus.
3. Hansel and Gretel lost their way. While watching for some birds.	3. Hansel and Gretel lost their way while watching for some birds.

Run-On Sentences	**Proper Sentences**
1. Venus is a planet we are studying in school it is many miles away.	1. Venus is a planet we are studying in school. It is many miles away.
2. The police were called they sped to the scene of the accident.	2. The police were called and they sped to the scene of the accident.
3. The reading was very difficult, the assignment impossible.	3. The reading was very difficult, so the assignment was impossible.

Directions: Read the following paragraph. Try to identify any sentence fragments and run-on sentences.

Collecting antiques is an enjoyable and profitable hobby for a growing number of people today. Many people who are seriously interested in history. Collect everything from books to buttons. These kinds of items give us direct contact with the ideas and customs of past generations. That they represent. Other people get pleasure from collecting old furniture, it is often more useful and better built than modern furniture. In addition, there are some people who collect anything old. When they hear about some antiques selling for hundreds or thousands of dollars, they look for *any* item that might bring them a windfall. In short, more and more people are collecting antiques for fun and profit.

Assignment: With a small group, discuss some of the problems found in the paragraph and think of different ways these problems could be corrected. Rewrite the paragraph correcting any sentence fragments and run-on sentences.

SENTENCE VARIETY I

Information: Some people write paragraphs consisting mainly of simple sentences. Others use mostly compound or complex sentences. An excellent way to improve your writing style would be to use a variety of sentence types in your paragraphs.

Directions: Read and compare Paragraphs A and B. Then answer the questions that follow.

Paragraph A

The sun is our best energy resource of the future. First, our supplies of natural gas, oil, and coal are not endless. However, it seems our supply of solar energy would be sufficient for eons. Nuclear energy could be used for centuries, but we are all aware of the dangers of radioactivity and waste products. Another source of energy is electricity, yet we need coal or oil to produce it. In conclusion, the best part about solar energy is that we don't have to produce it. We only have to learn how to harness the abundant supply of it.

Paragraph B

The sun is our best energy resource of the future. Our supplies of natural gas, oil, and coal are not endless. Nuclear energy could be used for a long time. There are dangerous waste products and radiation involved in the production of nuclear energy. Electricity is a clean fuel. Plants need either coal or oil to manufacture it. We don't have to make solar power. The sun has an abundant supply of it. We could use it forever.

1. How are Paragraphs A and B similar? _____

2. How are Paragraphs A and B different? _____

3. Which do you think is the better of the two? _____ Why? _____

_____

_____

Assignment: Discuss your answers with a small group of other students in your class. Then present your group's answers to the rest of the class.

SENTENCE VARIETY II

Directions: One way to check for sentence variety is to count the number of words per sentence. Another way is to check the sentence patterns. Read the paragraph below and answer the questions that follow.

Swimming is an activity that provides the best exercise for most people. Constant movement of arms, legs, and trunk make it a total body exercise. Most of the body's muscles are therefore working at the same time. Swimming is different from other types of exercises like running and bicycling. It does not jar the bones or cause damage to knees and ankles. Also, it seldom stretches or pulls muscles, cartilage, or tendons. I think swimming is the best total exercise for people of all ages.

1. How many sentences are in the paragraph? _____ Count the number of words per sentence and list here:

   _____

   _____

   _____

2. Could you improve the variety of sentences by changing the length of sentences in a paragraph? _____
   Why or why not? _____

   _____

   _____

   _____

3. What sentence pattern (subject/predicate; predicate/subject) is used in each sentence? _____

   _____

   _____

   _____

4. Could you improve the paragraph by changing the sentence patterns? Why or why not? _____

   _____

   _____

   _____

Assignment: Rewrite the paragraph. Use a variety of sentence patterns, including signal words, and vary sentence lengths.

DETAILS UNRELATED TO TOPIC

Directions: Read the following paragraph. Try to identify any problems that may be present.

Our sources of energy are rapidly decreasing, yet we are so wasteful. In the first place, some people drive their cars unnecessarily and without any purpose. Second, supplies of natural gas are so scarce in some states that schools and factories must close during part of the winter months. At the same time, people in other states refuse to help by turning down their thermostats. A friend of my brother has a fireplace, but he doesn't even use it. How many people do you know who waste energy by playing the television too long or leaving the lights on when they aren't needed? Also, we should stop buying oil from foreign countries because we will become too dependent on them. Finally, because the world's population is increasing so rapidly, we need to conserve our present supplies for the future.

Check any problem areas found in the paragraph. Be ready to support your answer.

_____introductory statement   _____sentence variety

_____mechanics (spelling, grammar, etc.) _____details not related to topic

_____concluding statement   _____word choice

Assignment: Look at the topics listed below. Each has a list of possible details that might support the introductory statement. However, some of the details are *unrelated* to the topic. Put an X on the line next to these unrelated details. Then write a paragraph on one of the topics.

Fiction is my favorite kind of reading material.	Of all seasons, summer is the most entertaining.	Teenagers should earn their own spending money.
____characters like Paul Bunyan and Pecos Bill	____stay around the house	____some kids don't know math
____biographies of famous Americans	____picnic in the park	____will help keep kids busy and out of trouble
____poems are fun, too	____swim at the lake	____parents need free time
____events not real, but it's interesting to pretend	____wait for school to close for holidays	____teaches how to handle money
____songs are poems put to music	____play ball with friends	____my brother and sister have jobs

REDUNDANCY (REPEATING IDEAS)

Directions: Read the following paragraph. Try to identify any problems that may be present.

The cafeteria service and menu at our school is really outstanding. The workers are always courteous and helpful when we file through the line. Although some students do not exactly use the best of manners, the cafeteria staff is always helpful and polite. Most days the menu is both nutritious and tasty. My favorite is pizza day, even though I could eat more than the small slice they give us. There always seems to be a balance of the four food groups in each day's meal and those meals are usually delicious. Furthermore, the meals are nutritious and good tasting, especially the salad and pizza they serve on Friday. In summary, I believe our cafeteria staff prepares excellent meals and serves them with the skill of true professionals.

Check any problem areas found in the paragraph. Be ready to support your answer.

_____ introductory statement	_____ mechanics	_____ organization
_____ concluding statement	_____ word choice	_____ sentence variety
_____ redundancy	_____ details not related to topic	_____ other

Information: You have probably noticed that two ideas were repeated in the paragraph. How do you prevent this common problem in students' writing? Two suggestions are given below that may help to eliminate redundancy.

1. Organize your ideas or notes *before* you begin to write. In this way, you can see how many *different* ideas you have.

2. Proofread your first draft carefully, looking for any ideas that are the same. Even though you may have used different words, you may still be repeating the same idea.

Assignment: Revise and rewrite the paragraph. Make any improvements you feel are necessary.

PRO/CON APPROACH I

Information: When discussing a controversial issue, there is usually a clear choice: either you agree and support a position (pro), or you disagree and reject it (con). Using the pro/con approach, you should first identify the audience and purpose. Then list some examples or reasons and any supporting details on *both* sides of the issue. Finally, organize those notes into several paragraphs to persuade the audience to accept your opinion.

Directions: Read the situation and the notes that follow.

Situation: The Assistant Superintendent in your school system has recommended to the Board of Education that it change its current policy and require all high school students to complete eighteen credits for graduation. Currently, only sixteen credits are required. Due to a heated discussion at a recent Board meeting, the recommendation was postponed until further information could be obtained. Students have been asked to write their opinions on this issue and present them at the next meeting.

Audience _____

Purpose _____

Notes

Pro	Con
more learning will take place decreases number of study halls improves overall educational system better preparation for future	those students leaving for Occupational Education or Work Study Program will not have time requires more teachers and more money less time for special help to many students

Assignment: Using either the "pro" or "con" notes, write several paragraphs to persuade the Board of Education to accept your opinion. Be sure to:

1. State your opinion clearly.

2. Explain your reasons carefully.

3. Revise before writing the final draft.

PRO/CON APPROACH II

Directions: Read the situation and identify the audience and purpose. Then list your notes (both pro and con) in the spaces provided.

Situation: Even though you are an above-average swimmer, you still feel a need to improve your skills. Therefore, you want to attend a three-week competitive swim camp this summer. Your parents are questioning this request because of the cost ($200 fee, plus daily transportation). Write to your parents explaining why you want to attend.

Audience

Purpose

Notes

Pro	Con

Assignment: Write several paragraphs to your parents stating your opinion, giving at least two reasons or examples for that opinion, and details that support those reasons. Be sure to:

1. State your opinion clearly.

2. Explain your reasons carefully.

3. Revise before writing the final draft.

PROBLEM/SOLUTION APPROACH I

Information: You are sometimes asked to respond to a particular problem that has no clear-cut answer. In this case, a problem is stated and you must offer a solution to it.

Although you must still identify your audience and purpose, your notes may vary slightly from the "for/against" or "pro/con" format. You should list as many solutions to the problem as possible. Then expand two or three of those by listing specific examples and details that support your solution. Finally, select the solution that best supports your position.

Directions: Read the situation and look at the notes that follow.

Situation: The principal of your school has asked members of the student body to suggest one way in which school life could be improved. Those ideas that are clearly written and supported will be considered. Explain at least two reasons how or why your idea would improve school life.

Notes

1. Expand the intramural sports program

   a. will involve more students in athletic program, especially those not good enough for varsity sports
   b. may give some students better preparation for varsity competition
   c. may reduce the number of athletic teams, thereby saving the district money

2. Provide short-term mini-courses to students

   a. could take the place of many study halls and reduce wasted time
   b. students might teach others their hobbies or interests
   c. no credit or grades would be given

Assignment: Choose one of the two suggestions listed above—or one of your own—and expand it into several paragraphs. Be sure to:

1. State your opinion clearly.

2. Explain your reasons carefully.

3. Revise before writing the final draft.

PROBLEM/SOLUTION APPROACH II

Directions: Read the situation and identify the audience and purpose. Then list your notes in the space provided.

Situation: The school district's cafeteria program operated in the red last year, showing a net loss of $23,284. Next year there will be a 15% decrease in government aid, amounting to an additional $31,759 loss to the district. There has been considerable discussion in the district about this problem and the Board of Education has asked students for their opinion on possible solutions.

Audience ————————————————————

Purpose ————————————————————

Notes

Assignment: Using your notes, write to the Board of Education stating your solution. Give at least two reasons or examples for that solution and details that support the reasons. Be sure to:

1. State your opinion clearly.

2. Explain your reasons carefully.

3. Revise before writing the final draft.

PERSUASIVE WRITING: COUNTERING TECHNIQUE I

Directions: A very effective way to enhance your opinion is to counter the arguments of the opposing viewpoint. Read the statements below and answer the questions that follow.

    A. <u>I realize you</u> want me to continue my education next year. <u>However,</u> I feel the need to discontinue school and work for a year or two.

    B. <u>Even though</u> you feel Senator Adams is more experienced, <u>let me explain</u> how Mr. Burnett's background makes him a better candidate.

    C. <u>I understand you believe</u> urban renewal is the best answer to better housing and neighborhoods. <u>On the other hand,</u> have you considered how urban renovation would be a less costly and more effective solution?

1. How does the writer begin each paragraph? _____

_____

_____

2. Do you think this is an effective technique? _____ Why or why not?

_____

_____

Information: You should see from the examples above that the writer knows the opponent's position and attempts to reject the argument with a solid counter-argument. This technique informs your audience that you have already considered the reason and have decided to reject it.

Remember that in order to make your "counter" effective, you must expand the paragraph to include reasons or examples and supporting details. Otherwise, your viewpoint will be no more convincing than the one you are countering.

Assignment: Either in groups, pairs, or individually develop *one* of the examples listed above. Fully explain your position with reasons or examples and supporting details.

PERSUASIVE WRITING: COUNTERING TECHNIQUE II

Information: If used properly, the countering technique can be a very effective way to present your opinion on an issue. The opposing viewpoint is considered, but is quickly rejected in favor of your position. Supporting details, examples, and reasons should make your opinion very persuasive.

Directions: Read the signal words listed in the box below. They may help you when countering the arguments of the opposing viewpoint. Add to the list when you think of additional signals.

I realize you ...	believe	but,
I understand you ...	feel	yet,
Even though you ...	maintain	however,
Although you ...	want	I doubt ...
Some people ...	support	I question ...
Your idea to____deserves	favor	Let me explain ...
some merit	argue	On the other hand ...
It may be that you ...	state	On the contrary ...
		Nevertheless ...

Assignment: Read the topic ideas and audiences listed below and write three topic sentences (one or two sentences per topic) using the countering technique. An example is given.

Topic Ideas	Audiences
smoking	parent
legal voting age	teacher
military draft	another student
use of public facilities	principal
changes in school policy	board of education
homework assignment	lawmaker
testing	editor of local newspaper

Example: Congressman Johnson feels all 18-year-old men and women should be required to serve their country in the military draft. I question whether *military* service is appropriate for both men and women.

1. _____

_____

_____

2. _____

_____

_____

3. _____

_____

_____

PERSUASIVE WRITING: COUNTERING TECHNIQUE III

Directions: Read the situation and identify the audience and purpose. Then organize your notes for both sides of the issue.

Situation: Your parents are deciding whether or not to enforce a weekend curfew of midnight for you. They want your opinion on this matter. Decide whether you think the curfew is necessary or not.

Audience _____

Purpose _____

Notes

For	Against

Assignment: Using the countering technique and the signal words, write several paragraphs to your parents stating your opinion, giving at least two reasons or examples for that opinion, and details that support those reasons. Be sure to:

1. State your opinion clearly.

2. Counter the opposing point of view in the topic sentences.

3. Explain your reasons carefully.

4. Revise before writing the final draft.

PRACTICE AND REVIEW I

Directions: Read the situation and identify the audience and purpose. Then determine whether it is a "pro/con" or a "problem/solution" type of situation. Next, organize your notes in the box.

Situation: The mayor of Blackwell is deciding whether or not to have the town sponsor monthly Saturday night dances for teenagers at the Recreation Center. She wants opinions from several groups in the community, including the teenagers who live in Blackwell. Write to the mayor expressing your opinion on this issue.

Audience _____

Purpose _____

Type of Situation _____

Notes

_____

Assignment: Write several paragraphs to the mayor stating your opinion, giving at least two reasons or examples for that opinion, and details that support those reasons. Be sure to:

1. State your opinion clearly.

2. Explain your reasons carefully.

3. Revise before writing the final draft.

PRACTICE AND REVIEW II

Directions: Read the situation and identify the audience and purpose. Then determine whether it is a "pro/con" or a "problem/solution" type of situation. Next, organize your notes in the box.

Situation: Each year, your school district adds extra days to school calendar to guard against the loss of time due to weather or emergency conditions. The state requires each district to be in session a minimum of 180 days. Your school had 183 days scheduled this year, with none of the emergency days used. Write to your principal expressing your opinion on what should be done with the extra three days.

Audience⎯⎯⎯⎯⎯⎯⎯⎯⎯⎯⎯⎯⎯⎯⎯⎯⎯⎯⎯⎯⎯⎯⎯⎯⎯⎯⎯⎯⎯

Purpose⎯⎯⎯⎯⎯⎯⎯⎯⎯⎯⎯⎯⎯⎯⎯⎯⎯⎯⎯⎯⎯⎯⎯⎯⎯⎯⎯⎯⎯

Type of Situation⎯⎯⎯⎯⎯⎯⎯⎯⎯⎯⎯⎯⎯⎯⎯⎯⎯⎯⎯⎯⎯⎯⎯⎯

Notes

Assignment: Write several paragraphs to the principal stating your opinion, giving at least two reasons or examples for that opinion, and details that support those reasons. Be sure to:

1. State your opinion clearly.

2. Explain your reasons carefully.

3. Revise before writing the final draft.

PRACTICE AND REVIEW III

Directions: Read the situation and identify the audience and purpose. Then determine whether it is a "pro/con" or a "problem/solution" type of situation. Next, organize your notes in the box.

Situation: An out-of-town rock group known as "Shows Unlimited" has contacted A.J. Brocker, a local farmer. The group wants to rent his 750-acre farm for the weekend of July 4 in order to have a rock concert. Although Mr. Brocker is agreeable to this, the Town Council must decide whether or not to allow this event to take place. There is quite a bit of disagreement on this topic, both on the Council and in the community. Write to the Town Council to convince them of your opinion.

Audience _____

Purpose _____

Type of Situation _____

Notes

Assignment: Write several paragraphs to the Town Council stating your opinion, giving at least two reasons or examples for that opinion, and details that support those reasons. Be sure to:

1. State your opinion clearly.

2. Explain your reasons carefully.

3. Revise before writing the final draft.

PRACTICE AND REVIEW IV

Directions: Read the situation and identify the audience and purpose. Then determine whether it is a "pro/con" or a "problem/solution" type of situation. Next, organize your notes in the box.

Situation: The Town Council is concerned about the rising costs of energy and the effect of those increases on the city budget. An Energy Conservation Committee has been formed to brainstorm alternatives for reducing energy consumption. This committee, among other efforts, has contacted all city schools asking students for their ideas. As a concerned student, write to the committee expressing your opinion on what could be done.

Audience————————————————————

Purpose————————————————————

Type of Situation————————————————————

Notes

Assignment: Write several paragraphs to the committee stating your opinion, giving at least two reasons or examples for that opinion, and details that support those reasons. Be sure to:

1. State your opinion clearly.

2. Explain your reasons carefully.

3. Revise before writing the final draft.

PRACTICE AND REVIEW V

Directions: Read the situation and identify the audience and purpose. Then determine whether it is a "pro/con" or "problem/solution" type of situation. Next, organize your notes in the box.

Situation: Your state assemblyman has sponsored Bill No. 27004 that, if it becomes law, would prohibit the sale of nonreturnable bottles and cans in your state. The bill would require that every can or bottle be "taxed" five cents. This charge would then be returned to the consumer when the bottles or cans were returned. As a concerned consumer and state resident, let your assemblyman know how you feel about this issue.

Audience _____

Purpose _____

Type of Situation _____

Notes

Assignment: Write several paragraphs to the assemblyman stating your opinion, giving at least two reasons or examples for that opinion, and details that support those reasons. Be sure to:

1. State your opinion clearly.

2. Explain your reasons carefully.

3. Revise before writing the final draft.

PRACTICE AND REVIEW VI

Directions: Read the situation and identify the audience and purpose. Then determine whether it is a "pro/con" or "problem/solution" type of situation. Next, organize your notes in the box.

Situation: Your school has recently had a rash of vandalism in vacant classrooms, lavatories, and other unsupervised areas. Although the administration has caught and punished several students, they are unable to stop all of this unexplainable destruction. They are considering very drastic action that would really punish *all* students. Therefore, they have asked the Student Council to propose solutions to the problem that might not be so drastic. As a member of the Student Council, write to the administration with your opinion on this issue.

Audience _____

Purpose _____

Type of Situation _____

Notes

Assignment: Write several paragraphs to the administration stating your opinion, giving at least two reasons or examples for that opinion, and details that support those reasons. Be sure to:

1. State your opinion clearly.

2. Explain your reasons carefully.

3. Revise before writing the final draft.

PRACTICE AND REVIEW VII

Directions: Read the situation and identify the audience and purpose. Then determine whether it is a "pro/con" or "problem/solution" type of situation. Next, organize your notes in the box.

Situation: The Metropolitan Gas and Electric Corporation has purchased property in your area specifically for the purpose of constructing a nuclear power plant. A public forum has been scheduled to discuss this issue. As a concerned citizen and resident, you intend to present your views at the meeting, which is sponsored by the city council members. Write your opinion to read at the meeting.

Audience _____

Purpose _____

Type of Situation _____

Notes

Assignment: Write several paragraphs to present at the meeting stating your opinion, giving at least two reasons or examples for that opinion, and details that support those reasons. Be sure to:

1. State your opinion clearly.

2. Explain your reasons carefully.

3. Revise before writing the final draft.

PERSUASIVE WRITING: OUTLINE FORM

Topic _____

Audience _____

Purpose _____

Trigger Words

money	safety	friendship	education	responsibility
time	energy	equality	environment	transportation
health	danger	pleasure	cooperation	conservation

Introductory Statement _____

_____

Opinion _____

_____

Reason #1 _____

_____

Details _____

_____

_____

Reason #2 _____

_____

Details _____

_____

_____

Reason #3 _____

_____

Details _____

_____

_____

Concluding Statement _____

_____

Conclusion _____

_____

PERSUASIVE WRITING TOPICS

1. Watching television is a waste of time.

2. Parents do not listen to (or talk to) their children enough.

3. Girls should (or should not) be permitted to participate on boys' athletic teams.

4. The best way to forget your troubles is to _____.

5. No one should be allowed to hunt unless he or she is at least 25 years old and has completed a hunter safety course.

6. People are born good; society makes them bad.

7. How a student behaves should not affect his or her grades.

8. At age 18, all young men and women should be required to serve their country for one year.

9. A college education is not for everyone.

10. A person needs many friends in order to feel needed and part of a group.

PERSUASIVE WRITING: SIGNAL WORDS

Introductory Phrases

In my opinion	There is no doubt that	I question whether
I believe	From my point of view	I (dis)agree with
It is my belief that	It seems to me that	I maintain that

Concluding Phrases

For the reasons above	To sum up	In short	In brief
As you can see	To be sure	Undoubtedly	In any event
As I have noted	Without a doubt	In conclusion	In any case
In other words	In summation	Obviously	Concluding
On the whole	Unquestionably	Summarizing	

Supporting Opinions

First	Furthermore	Equally important	Besides	Further
Second	In addition	In the first place	Next	Again
Third	Also	Likewise	Moreover	Similarly
Finally	Last			

Introducing Details

For example	For instance	In support of this
In fact	As evidence	

Cause and Effect

Since	Caused by	In effect
Because of	This results in	Brought about
Due to	Consequently	Made possible
For this reason	Accordingly	As might be expected
Therefore	As a result of	Give rise to
If ... then	Leads to	Was responsible for

Compare and Contrast

Similarly	Likewise	As well as	Whether or not
Compared to	In the same way	Have in common	Even though
In like manner	Contrasting	All are	Rather than
On the other hand	On the contrary	The same as	Nevertheless
Although	As opposed to	Conversely	In spite of

Countering

I realize you	believe	but
I understand you	feel	yet
Even though you	maintain	however
Although you	want	I doubt
Some people	favor	I question
It may be that you	support	Let me explain
Your idea to____deserves	argue	On the other hand
some merit	state	On the contrary
		Nevertheless

ANSWER KEY

PW 1

1. Lions are the best team.
2. four.
3. allowed fewer yards per game; gave up only eight touchdowns in twelve games.
4. There is no doubt ...
5. In conclusion ...
6. In the first place, they have the most explosive offense in the league. Also, the Lions' defense is outstanding. Furthermore, when the score is close and the end is near, the Lions always deliver that clutch play to win the game. In conclusion, if the evidence presented above does not convince you that the Lions are best in the league, then let their 12-0 record speak for itself.
7. Yes. It includes four reasons plus supporting details.

PW 2

Answers will vary. Sample:
For Fast-Food Program:
      pays attention to students' likes and dislikes
      tastes better
      no wasted food
      better service
For Present Cafeteria Program:
      less expensive
      better variety
      more nutritious
      wastes less paper products

I favor the present cafeteria program over a fast-food service program. In the first place, the present system is less expensive. I couldn't buy a complete fast-food lunch for the 75¢ I now spend on school lunches. In addition, the cafeteria offers a daily variety of food, not just the same menu of hamburgers, hot dogs, french fries, and soda. Furthermore, the present lunches are more nutritious. The cafeteria must, by law, provide portions of all the basic food groups at each meal. As you can see, the present system should be continued. It's much more nutritious, offers a wider variety of food, and is much less expensive. There is also less waste of paper products.

PW 3

Answers will vary. Sample:
Reasons for:
> should not discriminate between sexes
> women do not have to perform more physical duties
> necessary to keep military strong
> patriotism
> responsibility
> provides good training
> other countries include women

Reasons Against:
> most women not able to perform some duties, especially combat
> could be illegal, especially during peacetime
> volunteers can keep military strong
> not fair to those still going to school
> not fair to those raising families
> those forced into service don't perform so well

I feel there should be a military draft for both men and women over 18 years of age in the United States. The most important reason is the need to keep our country strong defensively, and I don't feel a volunteer system can provide the quantity and quality of people needed for a strong military. I also feel strongly that both men and women should participate in the draft. Obviously, women may not be capable of performing certain duties, but most positions could be filled just as effectively by women. Finally, I favor a military draft because it is our patriotic duty and responsibility to serve our country in some way. In conclusion, I feel a military draft for all 18 year olds is a sound idea and the reasons above support this conclusion.

PW 4

1. Audience: parents. Purpose: to persuade them to let you buy a used car.
2. Audience: City Council. Purpose: to state opinion about 9:30 p.m. curfew.
3. Audience: principal. Purpose: to describe two problems and offer solutions.

Answers will vary. Sample:

Since I have recently received my driver's license, and since I have saved several hundred dollars, I would like to buy a used car. Before making a decision, let me explain two reasons why this would be a good idea.

How many times during the week do I ask you for the family car to taxi me and the other kids around town? It seems there is always a conflict in arranging schedules so everyone can make their meetings, clubs, and practices. If I had a car, that problem would be reduced greatly. In addition, I could get to and from my part-time job without having either of you drive me back and forth. Think of how convenient that would be!

You are probably thinking it would be an added expense. However, I make enough money in my job to pay for any extra insurance, maintenance, and gasoline expenses. In fact, we might save money by decreasing the extra wear and tear on our family car. Furthermore, I would agree to let other members of the family use the car when I don't need it. In a way, this would be a second family car.

I realize this request must be a surprise to you. When you think of the advantages, allowing me to buy a car would be helpful and convenient to everyone. I hope you'll consider these as you make your decision.

PW 5

1. Audience in Paragraph A: a legislator or lawmaker.
   Audience in Paragraph B: school administration or Board of Education.
2. Purpose of Paragraph A: to persuade a legislator.
   Purpose of Paragraph B: to persuade educational leaders.
Answers will vary. Sample:

The proposal to change the legal driving age from sixteen to eighteen years of age in our state has several drawbacks. Your editorials supporting this proposal have not considered two very important consequences. In the first place, raising the age will cause undue hardships for older teenagers who drive to after-school activities or part-time jobs. In fact, many teens are seventeen when they graduate from high school. How will they get to their jobs without driver's licenses? Also, think about the added expenses to local school districts. In our school there are almost 150 students who rely on private transportation to and from school. Most of these travel in student-driven cars. If the age were raised, the school district would have to supply transportation for all those extra students. The added expenses for more buses and more gasoline would be a considerable expense statewide. I urge you to consider these arguments and present them to your readers.

PW 6

Answers will vary. Samples:
1. Audience: Board of Education.
   Purpose: Don't cut sports programs.

As a student at this school, I have looked forward to the day when I could play varsity tennis. Now I hear that several sports, including girls' tennis, will be cut next year. I oppose this action. Varsity competition is an extremely important part of a school's overall program. It gives us the opportunity to exercise, to socialize with friends outside of the classroom, and to help develop a positive school spirit. Not only that, interscholastic sports let us meet and compete against students from other schools. I hope you will reconsider and cut the budget in other areas so that the present program remains.
2. Audience: Friend.
   Purpose: Explain situation and request support.

You won't believe what the Board of Education wants to do! They want to drop several varsity sports—including girls' tennis. You sure were lucky to have graduated last year. As you know, I've waited two years to start on the team, and after all that time and practice, it's going to be cut. I'll miss the exercise, the competition, and most of all the team spirit. If you have a chance, will you please write to the Board of Education expressing how important sports were to you? Maybe it will help them change their minds!

PW 7

Answers will vary. Samples:
1. In my opinion, students are often accused of cheating so much in school, but notice how much adults cheat in their everyday lives.
2. There is no doubt that physical fitness is important to a person's good mental and physical health.
3. I maintain that going steady is an important part of growing up.

   In my opinion, students are often accused of cheating so much in school, but notice how much adults cheat in their everyday lives. A perfect example is the way adults try to lower their income taxes. Just listen to them talk about how they increased a deduction or didn't claim all of their income. Another example involves some of our political leaders. Not a month goes by when we don't hear of a congressman taking kickbacks or an assemblyman accepting favors for voting a certain way. Maybe if adults didn't try to cheat so much, students wouldn't follow their example.

PW 8

Answers will vary. Sample:
1. the class officers.
2. to suggest how the class will spend its money.
3. to start a scholarship fund for a graduating senior.
4. a. to help needy student finance education.
   b. spend money on others rather than ourselves.

   In my opinion, our class should use the $1,400 in our treasury to start a scholarship fund for a graduating senior's higher education. In the first place, there is at least one person every year who wants to attend college or some other school, but he or she can't afford it. This amount may be enough to give that person the opportunity to further his or her education. Furthermore, if our class establishes this fund, maybe future classes will do the same. We have always spent the treasury money on dances or other events that are here today and gone tomorrow. For once, let's do something for someone else. I think all of us will benefit.

PW 9

Information: organizing; opinion.
Directions: four; second, third, fourth, fifth sentences; The present, Some students, Salad lunches, When students.
Answers will vary. Sample:

   In my opinion, the school cafeteria should offer a salad bar as well as the hot lunch counter already available. In the first place, the present hot lunches are starchy and fattening.

Also, some students would probably waste less food because they would only serve themselves what they really like. In addition, salad lunches don't give you that slow, heavy feeling that makes it difficult to work in the afternoon. Moreover, when students are served tray lunches they eat only what they like, so they probably don't get a very balanced meal. For the reasons above, you can probably understand why I feel a salad bar should be offered as part of our cafeteria menu.

PW 10

Answers will vary. Samples:
1. I would like the opportunity to visit John at his college Spring Weekend in College City.
2. friendship. John is my good friend and it would be a good chance to visit him.
3. pleasure. I have worked hard all year. It would be a break from schoolwork and part-time job. I deserve a special vacation.
4. responsibility. I've seldom been away from home. I'm responsible enough to behave myself and still have a fun-filled weekend.

I would like the opportunity to visit my friend, John, at his college Spring Weekend. As you know, John is a good friend of mine and we have not had much time to see each other since he went away to school. After working so hard this past year in school and at my job, I think I deserve a break to enjoy myself. Also, you always tell me I must learn to be more responsible. I've seldom been away from home and I think I'm old enough and responsible enough to have a fun-filled weekend and still be mature. I hope you will allow me to attend this weekend. I believe I deserve a break to visit my friend, while at the same time show you how responsible I am.

PW 11

Directions: A; It gives specific details (3 deaths, 35 accidents, 20 complaints, fences knocked down) to support the reasons.
Assignment: notes; organize; opinion.
Answers will vary. Sample:

I think homework is a waste of time. If a student has a question about the assignment, no one can answer, assist, or guide her with it. Therefore, the student may misunderstand the homework and become frustrated or discouraged. The most convincing argument against homework is that so many students don't bother to do it. Consequently, the teacher spends extra class time just to yell at the lazy ones. Those of us who did bother with the homework are forced to listen to this. I admit there are times when homework is a valuable activity, but most of the time it is a waste of time.

PW 12

Answers will vary. Sample:
When? there's not enough snow on the ground; conditions are poor.

Where? in people's yards; on farmers' fields; unfamiliar areas.
Who or What? inexperienced drivers; untrained drivers; farmers and landowners complain.
What kind of? inconsiderate; foolish; disrespectful.
Why? don't understand consequences; very heavy; tracks chew up soil.
What happens? damages some crops; rips up lawns; breaks fences.

Snowmobiles are destructive to property, especially if these heavy machines are driven without enough snow on the ground or when weather conditions are poor. Ask any farmer who has seen the results of inexperienced, untrained drivers whose snowmobile's tracks have left paths of mud in winter wheat fields. Or, talk to homeowners whose lawns have been torn up. Some inconsiderate and disrespectful drivers even cut down or run over fences to avoid hazards or take shortcuts. Yes, snowmobiles are destructive to property, and these are but a few examples to support my opinion.

PW 13

Answers will vary. Sample:
You can see that horse racing is an exciting form of entertainment for me, from its very beginning to its thrilling completion.

PW 14

Answers will vary. Sample:
Opinion: It is a good idea not to let students leave classrooms except for emergencies.
Reasons: 1. no immediate need to be in halls during class time, except for an emergency
      2. have plenty of time to take care of personal needs in between classes.
      3. will help cut down thefts
Solution: will be unpopular, so try on trial basis and compare results.

In summary, Mr. Howard, I agree with your decision to restrict hallway activity during class periods. Most hallway travel during class time is unnecessary and students can take care of most personal needs between classes. I would be eager to compare results of this new policy after it has been in effect about a month.

PW 15

Areas checked: spelling, grammar, capitalization, punctuation, words omitted, other.
I prefer to live in the country rather than the city for several reasons. There is less air pollution in the country because there are fewer cars and factories to spew poisonous hydrocarbons into the air. Also, country living is superior because of the extra land available to grow fresh fruits, vegetables, and flowers. Furthermore, everyone knows there is a lower crime rate in the country, so there will be less chance of someone hurting you. I guess you can understand why I prefer to live in the country.

PW 16

Areas checked: unrelated information, repetition of ideas, conclusion, other.

Year-round school calendars should be adopted in our state next year. When we close our schools for extended periods of time, we waste space. One result of this wasted space is wasted time. In addition, why spend thousands of dollars on expensive buildings if they aren't used 75-80 days per year? Besides, students get bored at home after ten days without school. Without a doubt, a year-round calendar for our state schools would save both space and money. I think we should adopt this policy.

PW 17

Answers will vary. Sample:

Some people think "camping out" means going to an electrified campsite in their $10,000 travel trailers. Their trailers include all the comforts of home, including soft beds, bathrooms, and heaters or air conditioners. These so-called campers own all the camping supplies to cook outdoors, but instead they go to the nearest store to buy prepared foods to cook on their stoves in the trailers. They even take along refrigerators and television sets.

To me, camping means going to an outside area where you can pitch a tent and cook a meal on an open fire, without hearing a television or radio blare. Walking to an area where animals roam free and talk to each other, and sleeping on the ground in a tent describe my idea of camping. In conclusion, camping should be a getaway from home, not a home away from home.

PW 18

Area checked: too choppy.
Answers will vary. Sample:

There is more to do with your spare time in the city than in the country. You can go to a big-league ball game or visit a museum, a zoo, or a park. I like going to the movies because there are so many from which you may choose in a big city. People live closer together, so there are more kids to play with. It is easier to travel around for all these activities as the transportation is excellent in the city. I really feel the city offers much more to do with your spare time.

PW 19

Answers will vary. Samples:
1. When John returns to work, Frank will be the boss. Frank will be the boss when John returns to work.
2. Since we had temperatures below freezing, my vegetables were destroyed. My vegetables were destroyed, since we had temperatures below freezing.
3. Because people were whispering to each other all around me, I could not concentrate on the speech. I could not concentrate on the speech because people were whispering to each other all around me.

4. Before you set up the tent behind the barn, I will make sure the owner gives us permission. I will make sure the owner gives us permission before you set up the tent behind the barn.

PW 20

Collecting antiques is an enjoyable and profitable hobby for a growing number of people today. Many people who are seriously interested in history collect everything from books to buttons. These kinds of items give us direct contact with the ideas and customs of past generations. Other people get pleasure from collecting old furniture because it is often more useful and better built than modern furniture. In addition, there are some people who collect anything old. When they hear about some antiques selling for hundreds or thousands of dollars, they look for any item that might bring them a windfall. In short, more and more people are collecting antiques for fun and profit.

PW 21

1. same information.
2. presented differently.
3. A; The sentence patterns are varied in Paragraph A. It uses signal words, and compound and complex sentences.

PW 22

1. seven. 12; 13; 12; 12; 13; 10; 13.
3. yes. Varying length will give the paragraph more rhythm.
3. subject/predicate; subject/predicate; subject/predicate; subject/predicate; subject/predicate subject/predicate; subject/predicate.
4. yes. Changing patterns makes it more interesting and provides more rhythm.

Answers will vary. Sample:

Swimming is an activity that provides the best exercise for most people. In the first place, constant movement of arms, legs, and trunk make it a total body exercise. Therefore, most of the body's muscles are working at the same time. Unlike running and bicycling, swimming does not jar the bones, cause damage to knees and ankles, or severely strain muscles, cartilage or tendons. You can see why I think swimming is the best total exercise for people of all ages.

PW 23

Area checked: details not related to topic.
Unrelated fiction details:

    biographies of famous Americans

    poems are fun, too

    songs are poems put to music

Unrelated summer details:
    stay around the house
    wait for school to close for holidays
Unrelated money details:
    some kids don't know math
    parents need free time
    my brother and sister have jobs
Answers will vary. Sample:

Of all the seasons, summer is the most entertaining. A picnic at a park is one activity I like. Cooking on a barbecue and eating with the whole family at a picnic table offers a welcome change from the normal meals at home. I also enjoy swimming at the lake, where I can spend hours on a warm summer day. Another entertaining activity is playing baseball with friends. We have a great time picking sides. Yes, summer is the most entertaining of the four seasons.

PW 24

Area checked: redundancy.
Answers will vary. Sample:

The cafeteria service and menu at our school are really outstanding. The workers are always courteous and helpful when we file through the line, even if some students don't exactly use the best of manners. Most days the menu is both nutritious and tasty. My favorite is pizza day, even though I could eat more than the small slice they give us. In addition, there always seems to be a balance of the four food groups in each meal. In summary, I believe our cafeteria staff prepares excellent meals and serves them with the skill of true professionals.

PW 25

Audience: Board of Education.
Purpose: to support their position on increasing credits required.
Answers will vary. Sample:

In my opinion, changing the number of credits required for graduation from sixteen to eighteen is an excellent idea. Even though this point of view may be unpopular with many students, I would like to explain two reasons why this action would improve our school's educational program.

In the first place, it will help prepare us for the future. For example, at the present time only two credits are required for math and science. With all of the current emphasis on technology, an extra course in math, science, and computer programming should benefit everyone. We would be better prepared for the job opportunities in all technical areas.

A big problem in our school is the amount of free time students have during the school day. Some students, especially juniors and seniors, are scheduled with two or three study halls every day because they only take the required three courses in English, Social Studies, and Health. This is a terrible waste of time! Increasing the number of credits would decrease the number of study halls, which don't aid learning at all.

On the whole, I think increasing the credits required for graduation would be a positive step forward. Not only would it help students prepare for the future, but it would also reduce the number of study halls and wasted time. More learning would take place and the overall educational system would improve greatly.

PW 26

Audience: parents.
Purpose: to convince parents to let you go to summer swim camp.
Answers will vary. Sample:

I would like the opportunity to attend the competitive swim camp this summer. Before you make a decision, let me explain some reasons why it would be a good idea.

You know how much I enjoy swimming and participating on the varsity swim team. The camp would be an excellent learning experience because I would improve my skills and be more competitive on next year's team. At the same time, I would meet and compete against some of the best swimmers in the state.

I know this camp would be an added expense, but it may be a good investment. I will be meeting several coaches at the camp and they could be influential in helping me find lifeguarding jobs in the future. Also, these coaches could help me get a swimming scholarship to a college in two more years. To meet the expenses this year, I would agree to pay you back and try to carpool with other students who plan to attend.

I hope you'll permit me to attend this swim camp. It means a lot to me and it may be a good investment for future jobs and a possible college scholarship.

PW 27

Answers will vary. Sample:

One suggestion that would greatly improve school life is an expanded intramural sports program. Although the present program is adequate, expansion will offer at least two advantages.

As far as students are concerned, intramurals should include activity in as many sports as possible. This year, only basketball and volleyball are offered. Many students don't like these two sports. Why not offer swimming, tennis, soccer, softball, and field hockey? Adding these sports could involve a greater number of students, especially those who are not good enough to participate at the varsity level. Of course, this would mean providing more time for sports. The new program should be held three or four days per week *all* year long, not just during the winter months.

Changing and expanding the present program might also interest the Board of Education because of cost savings. If the number of varsity and junior varsity teams were reduced, then less money would be spent on transportation, equipment, and officials. Some of this money could be applied to the expanded intramural program. Moreover, I sincerely believe more students would be active in athletics—just for the fun of it. A program that saves money and at the same time involves more students is a big improvement.

As you can see, Mr. Principal, expanded intramurals is a great way to improve school life. It would involve more students, more sports, and probably save money.

PW 28

Audience: Board of Education.
Purpose: to solve the cafeteria problem.
Answers will vary. Sample:

I believe the district's cafeteria system should be reduced next year to save the school district money. By completely changing the menu and services, thousands of dollars could be saved.

First of all, a number of time- and energy-consuming foods should be eliminated from the menu. They should be replaced with easy-to-prepare nutritious foods. For example, cooked vegetables and main courses are generally thrown away. On the other hand, uncooked fruits, vegetables, and salads can be refrigerated and offered for several days. Also, vending machines could be added. This practice would reduce both cafeteria staff and energy consumption.

Another system change might reduce preparation time and waste. If students declared in homeroom that they intended to buy a hot dish like soup, or a bag lunch, the cafeteria would not prepare extra food nor throw away as many leftovers.

In the end, I think this system would solve the problem without sacrificing cafeteria service and nutritious menus.

PW 29

1. by presenting the other viewpoint first.
2. yes. It acknowledges the opposite view and then rejects it.
Answers will vary. Sample:

I realize you want me to continue my education next year. However, I feel the need to discontinue school and work for a year or two. In the first place, I'm tired of school. I realize furthering my education is important, but I'm not really ready at this time. With that kind of attitude, I'm not likely to put forth my best effort. Another reason for delaying is that I haven't decided what profession to pursue. Working for a year or two will help me to decide. Besides, I would be able to save some money to apply toward this education. In conclusion, I hope you understand that I'm not yet ready to continue my studies. Delaying will give me the opportunity to decide on a profession and at the same time save some money toward preparing for it.

PW 30

Answers will vary. Samples:
1. I understand the Board of Education is concerned about insurance regulations when the school is used during vacations. On the other hand, nonuse of these public facilities for 70-80 days per year is a tremendous waste of money and space.
2. Mr. Principal, your idea to establish a smoking area for students deserves some merit. Let me explain why I feel this policy will not solve the smoking problem.
3. Even though you and the other legislators support a state testing program, I doubt whether this policy is necessary on a statewide level.

PW 31

Audience: parents.
Purpose: to convince them whether or not a weekend curfew of midnight is necessary.
Answers will vary. Sample:

In my opinion, a weekend curfew of 12 a.m. is not necessary. Let me explain a few reasons why this policy is unrealistic and unfair.

I realize you feel midnight is late enough, but many weekend events don't end until that time. For example, drive-in movies, school dances, and some other school activities don't end until almost midnight. Not only would I have to leave early, but I also wouldn't get a chance to go out for a late evening snack.

I know you are concerned with my whereabouts and I appreciate your concern. But you also know that I am responsible enough at my age to inform you where I will be, to drive carefully, and to come home at a reasonable hour.

Your concerns for a midnight curfew are well-founded. However, I think it is unfair and unrealistic to leave my friends and events early—especially if you know *where* I am. I hope you will trust my responsibility and not impose a midnight curfew.

PW 32

Audience: mayor of Blackwell.
Purpose: to express opinion on Saturday night dances.
Type of Situation: pro/con.
Answers will vary. Sample:

I strongly support the idea of town-sponsored, monthly Saturday night dances for teenagers in Blackwell. I know this opinion will be echoed by most other teenagers here for at least two reasons.

In a small town like Blackwell, there are so few activities for teenagers, especially when school is not in session. Dances at the Recreation Center will give us the chance to meet, listen to music, and dance. Since it is sponsored by the town, parents will allow their kids to attend. Consequently, these events will be well-attended.

Another advantage is less obvious, but quite important. Many teens don't trust or respect community leaders and other adults. Sponsoring dances proves to the doubting teens that adults are concerned about their welfare and do want to provide opportunities for enjoyment. Just this one action will do a lot to improve attitudes toward the community leadership.

Madame Mayor, I'm sure I speak for many teenagers when I urge you to sponsor these monthly dances at the Recreation Center. They will give us something extra to do and will also improve communication between adults and teenagers.

PW 33

Audience: principal.
Purpose: to explain what should be done with extra three days.
Type of situation: problem/solution.

Answers will vary. Sample:

In response to your request for a solution to the extra three days on the school calendar, I would like to suggest adding those days to the Memorial Day weekend. This move would solve a couple of problems.

Since absenteeism increases when the weather improves in late spring, adding the days to the Memorial Day weekend might give students a chance to vent their spring fever. Also, many families take vacations then, and students are usually absent illegally. Therefore, why not close school when absences are at a seasonal high?

Another advantage to adding those days in late May is to give students a needed break before the final exams. After a five-day holiday, students will be fresh and more inclined to better prepare themselves for the pressures of finals.

I'm sure many would agree, Mr. Principal, that adding the extra emergency days to the Memorial Day weekend would reduce illegal absences and get students in a refreshed frame of mind for the end of the school year.

PW 34

Audience: town council.
Purpose: to show if rock concert should take place on Brocker Farm.
Type of Situation: pro/con.
Answers will vary. Sample:

I realize A.J. Brocker is agreeable to renting his 750-acre farm to Shows Unlimited for a July 4 rock festival. However, I feel this event would pose several questions that should be answered before you make a decision.

The most obvious problem is safety. From all reports, this concert would attract more than 200,000 young people to our area. With all those people, there are likely to be traffic accidents, drug overdoses, or other medical emergencies. Since the nearest hospital is 30 miles away and since there will be so much traffic, a definite safety hazard would exist.

There are other questions which make it difficult to support this event. Can the community supply the extra food and water that number of people will use? Where will all those cars park? How can we provide bathroom facilities? Do we want to accept responsibility for local property damage and cleanup?

It seems to me there are many unanswered questions. Even though Mr. Brocker is willing to rent his farm, I think the problems outweigh the advantages. The Town Council should reject the proposal.

PW 35

Audience: Energy Conservation Committee.
Purpose: to explain how to reduce energy consumption.
Type of situation: problem/solution.
Answers will vary. Sample:

Since the Energy Conservation Committee has asked for ideas to help reduce energy consumption in our town, I have thought of two alternative measures which may be worthy of further study.

First, you might consider the possibility of installing automatic thermostat controls on all heating and cooling units in public buildings. These controls could be set at reasonable temperatures for normal working hours and nonworking hours. As a result, the units would work more efficiently. Also, individuals could not raise or lower temperatures whenever they were a bit uncomfortable.

Another action might involve more money and research, but it could pay back hundreds of thousands of dollars. Why not hire a geologist, or some other specialist, to study the land in our town and look for possible reserves of natural gas or oil? If we had our own supply of energy within the town, the savings could be astronomical.

I'm sure your committee has thought about energy-saving actions like increasing insulation and applying storm windows. However, I hope you will consider automatic thermostat controls in public buildings and searching for our own energy reserves of natural gas or oil.

PW 36

Audience: assemblyman.
Purpose: to give an opinion on Bill No. 27004.
Type of situation: pro/con.
Answers will vary. Sample:

No doubt the bill to prohibit the sale of nonreturnable bottles and cans will be inconvenient to some people in our state. It is my feeling, however, that Bill No. 27004 should be passed.

Traveling the state, county, and city roads can be very depressing. Everywhere I see stray bottles and cans littering our highways. Obviously some people don't attach any value to nonreturnables. If these containers had some value, people would be reluctant to throw them away, just as they wouldn't consider tossing nickels or dimes out the window. With a value placed on returnable bottles and cans, it would not take long for enterprising people to pick up after the foolish litterbugs.

Our society wastes so many things. Why can't we reuse glass bottles and recycle aluminum cans? Not only would we save raw materials, we would also reduce the energy costs of production. It just doesn't make sense to throw away things that can be used over and over again.

It seems silly to use nonreturnable cans and bottles just because they are convenient. Other states have passed similar laws. Why can't we recycle, reuse, and reduce the ugly litter?

PW 37

Audience: school administration.
Purpose: to explain what to do about vandalism.
Type of situation: problem/solution.
Answers will vary. Sample:

I agree that school vandalism is a growing problem, but I think we can attempt to solve it through student responsibility rather than negative administrative actions.

Students generally complain that the Student Council is a powerless and useless body. Why not let the Council establish a system to deal with vandalism? For example, let the Council and administration form a committee of responsible students to patrol the halls, lavatories, and other unsupervised areas during their free periods. They could easily report any problems to teachers or administrators. In addition, pairs of students could be assigned to empty classrooms for their study halls. In this way, extra faculty or security guards would not be required in these areas.

How many times do these vandals escape real punishment because their parents pay for the damages? They don't really care if they get caught because the penalties (suspension, paying back with someone else's money) are not applied properly. I believe that these vandals should be required to reimburse the school district with actual labor equal to the damage.

Punishing all students for the violations of a few is not really fair and may not solve the problem. But, if the students are involved in solving the problem, then I think the results will be much better.

PW 38

Audience: City Council members.
Purpose: to decide whether or not to construct a nuclear power plant.
Type of situation: pro/con.
Answers will vary. Sample:

I recognize the necessity and importance of nuclear power in the world, but I would like to propose to this forum that no new power plants be constructed.

In the first place, I'm concerned about the dumping of nuclear wastes. These nuclear byproducts will take hundreds of years to break down. In the meantime, where do all these wastes go? Can they be safely dumped anywhere and not present a potential health hazard? If we build more plants, there will only be more wastes to dispose of.

An additional safety hazard is the very real possibility of a nuclear accident. The near-meltdown at Three Mile Island in Pennsylvania and radiation leaks at the Ginna Plant near Rochester, New York are two examples. Even with the best precautions, nuclear accidents are possible.

In conclusion, I reject the proposal to build another nuclear power plant here or anywhere else. Safety hazards such as nuclear wastes and possible nuclear accidents are reason enough. Why not use the money that would be used for a nuclear power plant toward improving existing power plants and exploring alternative energy sources?

III

DESCRIPTIVE WRITING SKILLS AND ACTIVITIES

In contrast to practice in elementary schools, descriptive writing in the secondary schools tends to take a back seat to other forms of writing. Reporting information, analyzing literature and characters, and preparing for competency testing are usually emphasized. This section is included in the *Basic Composition Activities Kit* for three reasons. Descriptive writing skills contribute to facility in other types of writing, allow for more creativity in individual expression than other forms of writing, and give variety to the writing program.

Many of the activities in the descriptive writing section will aid the students' overall writing ability. Figurative language adds color, flavor, and zest. Appealing to the senses heightens detail and clarity. The various patterns of organization are reinforced. Moreover, the grammar and usage exercises found herein can be readily applied to those found in English textbooks.

To say that descriptive writing allows students "to do their own thing," unaided and without guidance, is not the purpose or intent of this unit. On the contrary, students—especially those needing basic composition instruction—need guidance, order, and structure. Just as carpenters need to plan and blueprint their houses, students must plan and outline their ideas. The Descriptive Writing Outline Form at the end of the unit (DW 34), along with adequate in-class prewriting activity, help students to organize their descriptive writing. Granted, they may alter their course midway through the writing, but the outline form and prewriting activity should supply enough support for students to succeed in descriptive writing.

III. DESCRIPTIVE WRITING SKILLS AND ACTIVITIES

STRUCTURING PARAGRAPHS

Information: A paragraph contains a group of closely related sentences, all dealing with a particular topic or idea. One sentence usually states the main idea of the paragraph. The others detail and describe whatever you want to say about it. You must remember two things about the paragraph:

1. The topic sentence must be one that makes a general statement about what will follow.

2. What follows must be directly related to that topic.

Directions: Read the following paragraph and answer the questions that follow.

My sixth-grade teacher, Miss Jackson, thought I was a troublemaker and I can only guess the reasons why. Maybe it was because I enjoyed laughing and playing practical jokes on my friends. One time I convinced a friend of mine to go to the office without Miss Jackson's knowledge. He got in trouble but never told on me. Since I was big for my age and my voice began to change, Miss Jackson probably felt I had repeated a grade or two. Therefore, I must have been a troublemaker in her eyes. I'm sure she sensed that I was not so interested in school work as I was in recess or gym because I always came to school with athletic equipment of some sort. Furthermore, a student always knows when the teacher doesn't trust him or her. Those eagle-eye stares and the pacing behind my desk were warnings enough of the distrust. I guess I'll never know the real reasons, but there's no doubt she thought I was a troublemaker.

1. What is the topic? _____

_____

_____

2. Is it stated clearly? _____

3. Are all of the details related to the topic? _____

4. Which details are not related to the topic? _____

_____

_____

_____

Assignment: Rewrite the paragraph. Eliminate those details that are not related to the topic. Add any details that might explain why the author was labeled a troublemaker.

WRITING INTRODUCTIONS

Information: The introduction of a descriptive paragraph is usually the topic sentence. Writing several different "leads" or beginnings is one way to compose a clear and effective topic statement. Simply choose the best one of those you have written.

Directions: Read the topic and the three introductions given below. Then answer the questions that follow.

Swimming Lessons

a. Since I don't like water very much, except for drinking and cleaning, I was pretty scared about attending my first swimming lessons at summer camp.

b. I was very nervous about my first swimming lessons at summer camp because my experiences with water were limited to drinking it or cleaning with it.

c. Because I had never gone swimming before, my first swimming lessons at summer camp were a frightening experience.

1. Which introduction do you like best?_____Why?_____

_____

_____

_____

2. What do you like or dislike about the other two?_____

_____

_____

_____

_____

_____

_____

_____

Assignment: Write three different introductions or "leads" to the topic "Household Pets" or any other topic you choose. Pick the best lead and write a descriptive paragraph about it.

KNOWING YOUR CONCLUSION

Information: Did you ever start with a good idea and not know how to end it? Many writers experience this problem. Some people write and write and suddenly end their writing without warning. Others think of an ending partway through and realize it won't make sense.

Some authors decide how their idea will end *before* they begin to write. Then they plot their way from beginning to end. This is an effective technique.

Directions: Read the topics below and their possible conclusions. Then write possible endings for the other topics listed.

Topic	Possible Conclusion
1. Vacation across country.	Returned home more tired than when I left.
2. Surprise birthday party.	Found out about it, but was surprised anyway when unexpected guests arrived.
3. First impression of a person.	_____
	_____
	_____
	_____
4. Moving to a new school.	_____
	_____
	_____
	_____
5. A hike through the woods.	_____
	_____
	_____
	_____
6. A subway ride.	_____
	_____
	_____
	_____

Assignment: Select one of the topics and its conclusion. Plan how you will go from start to finish. Write a descriptive paragraph (or paragraphs) on this topic.

USING ADJECTIVES

Information: It is hard to imagine writing descriptively without using adjectives. An adjective modifies, or describes, a noun or a pronoun. Notice the difference between the following sentences:

1. The bear climbed the tree looking for a beehive.

2. The huge grizzly bear climbed the maple tree looking for an abandoned beehive.

Obviously, the second sentence is far more interesting and precise in its description. Remember that the adjective would answer one of the following questions:

What kind? ... <u>hairy</u> beast, <u>pretty</u> butterfly
Which ones? ... <u>seventh</u> graders, <u>those</u> cars
How much? ... <u>three</u> pounds, <u>no</u> energy

Directions: Read the following paragraphs and fill in the blanks with descriptive adjectives. Do not use any adjective more than once.

I'll never forget the time my friends, the Ritter twins, and I decided to camp out in the _____ Cemetery. That was one of the _____ nights of my life. Before hiking down the _____ road to the entrance, we stopped at the _____ store to fill our pockets with _____ candy and _____ soda. Throwing our supplies over first, we then climbed the _____ gate and searched for a _____ place to bed down. No sooner had we settled down to tell _____ stories than the first _____ event happened. Simultaneously the moon disappeared and a _____ wind came upon us. What had been a _____ and _____ night was now _____ and _____.

Shortly thereafter, we heard what seemed to be a _____ accident on the road near the front entrance. But we continued reading _____ books with our flashlight and eating the treats we bought earlier. Then we heard a _____ sound, and a _____ light gradually came into focus. As it got closer, I saw Tim dart behind the large, _____ monument behind us. Paul and I bolted toward the _____ bushes to camouflage our presence. It seemed as though we were safe from this _____ sight, that is, until I saw Tim's flashlight shining directly at that _____ thing, which was slowly approaching us.

Assignment: Complete the story, using as many descriptive adjectives as possible.

AVOIDING VAGUE ADJECTIVES

Information: Because people use some adjectives so often and in so many ways, we really do not have an accurate or precise idea of what they mean. For example, read the following:

1. Barb said to Sue, "Bill really is a nice guy."

What does "nice" mean? Cute? Helpful? Friendly? It's difficult to understand exactly what is meant by the word "nice."

2. Frank thinks he is pretty big.

What does the adjective "big" mean? Important? Popular? Or does it mean he is "big" in size? If it refers to his size, then why not use "huge" or "enormous" or some other word that refers to size—not to personality.

Directions: Read the sentences below and in each one replace the underlined adjective with a more exact modifier. The new word should add interest and meaning to the noun and to the whole sentence.

1. I saw a <u>fantastic</u> movie Saturday night. _____

2. We think Mr. Sullivan is a <u>neat</u> person._____

3. If you touch an electric fence, you'll get
   a <u>weird</u> feeling.   _____

4. Your sister cooked a <u>great</u> supper.   _____

5. Betty is a <u>pretty good</u> student.   _____

Compare your answers with those of other students in the class. Notice how you probably used different adjectives than they did. In using different adjectives, you may have changed the whole meaning of the sentence.

Practice: Write your own adjectives in the spaces that follow. Compare yours to those of others in the class.

1. The hermit lived a _____ life in the woods.

2. Marie was a _____ student because no one really liked her.

3. We planted two _____ pine trees in our backyard.

4. After driving his motorcycle so fast, John learned a(n) _____ lesson.

5. My cousin has a _____ treehouse in her backyard.

6. No one is more _____ than Marcia when it comes to planning a party.

Assignment: Without using vague adjectives, write a story using the introductory statement given here. Use your imagination.

"I recently saw the most bizarre animal at the Bronx Zoo. It was called a Hiccalux and I'd like to tell you about it."

USING ACTION VERBS

Information: Most verbs—but not all—are words that express action. The use of action verbs helps us to write more descriptively. However some of these words are better than others because they paint a clearer picture of what we are describing. Read the sentences below. Note the underlined words and answer the questions that follow.

1. The road crew will <u>make</u> a tunnel under Mount Sienna.

2. Henry <u>said</u>, "I didn't forget to bring the forks!"

3. Joan really felt proud as she <u>went</u> home with a perfect report.

The action verbs <u>make</u>, <u>said</u>, and <u>went</u>, are examples of overworked and abused words. They could be replaced with more accurate action words. Cross out those three words in the sentences above and supply the sentences with better words.

Directions: Read Part One of the story below. Replace all underlined words with more action-packed verbs by crossing out the underlined word and writing the new word above it. When you finish, compare your answers with those of others in the class.

Backfire! Part One

I desperately wanted <u>to give</u> my brother a lesson, but <u>as it turned out</u>, I was the person who <u>got</u> the raw end of the deal. As the oldest of three boys, Richard <u>got</u> the attic for his bedroom. Steve and I always <u>said</u>, "That's not fair!" to our parents, but they never <u>gave in</u> to our demands for equality.

So, one day I <u>said</u> to myself, "I will just show him a thing or two!" I would like you to know that Richard had two bad habits that really <u>got to</u> me. First, he always <u>went</u> up and down the attic stairs like a herd of elephants. Second, he always <u>went</u> around barefoot, stinking up the room I happened to be in. Well, I <u>made</u> a plan. Off I went to the corner store that bright July afternoon to <u>get</u> some itching powder and thumbtacks.

Assignment: Conclude this story by writing Part Two. Use verbs that accurately describe the action.

USING ADVERBS

Information: Like adjectives, adverbs are also describing words. However adverbs modify a verb, an adjective, or another adverb. Look at the following examples:

1. The children <u>often</u> talked <u>nervously</u> when the principal was <u>there</u>.

   "Often" and "nervously" describe the verb "talked."
   "There" modifies the linking verb "was."
   An adverb can be located before *or* after the verb it modifies.

2. The <u>brightly</u> spotted guinea fowl <u>suddenly</u> disappeared.

   "Brightly" is an adverb and modifies the adjective "spotted."
   "Suddenly" is an adverb and modifies the verb "disappeared."
   "Suddenly" could be used at the beginning of the sentence.
   "Suddenly" could be used after the verb "disappeared."

3. The frightened boy ran <u>away instantly</u>.

   "Away" is an adverb and modifies the verb "ran."
   "Instantly" is an adverb and modifies the other adverb "away."

It is necessary to use adverbs regularly if you wish to write descriptively. How do you identify an adverb? Many end with the suffix "ly." However, all of them answer one of these questions:

<u>When</u>? (now, later, then, soon) . . . arrive <u>later</u>.
<u>Where</u>? (here, there) . . . threw <u>away</u>.
<u>How</u>? (calmly, patiently, quickly) . . . agree <u>wholeheartedly</u>.
<u>How often</u>? (always, sometimes) . . . <u>never</u> lie.
<u>To what degree</u>? (very, too, really) . . . <u>extremely</u> busy.

Directions: Read the following paragraph and fill in the blanks with descriptive adverbs. Do not use any word more than once.

The last time I visited the zoo was more than a year ago, but I can _____ remember everything I saw. Especially clear in my mind are the tigers and lions. They paced _____ around their cages _____ aware of the visitors who were watching them. The elephants also noticed our presence, because they _____ nibbled peanuts and salted crackers from our hands. _____ we watched the monkeys put on a show. Even my mother and father laughed _____ when the smallest one jumped _____ up and down, sticking his tongue out at us. By the time we arrived at the refreshment stand, our empty stomachs were growling _____. After lunch, we planned to visit many other interesting areas before the long trip home.

Assignment: Describe the remainder of the zoo visit, using descriptive adverbs whenever possible.

COMBINING SENTENCE FRAGMENTS

Information: Some writers have a tendency to write short, choppy sentences. These sentences can be expanded by answering such questions as When? Where? Why? How? What kind of?

Directions: Look at the following example.

A fire destroyed the Colonial Inn.
<u>What kind of</u>? A <u>raging</u> fire destroyed the <u>historic</u> Colonial Inn.
<u>Where</u>? A raging fire destroyed the historic Colonial Inn <u>in Waterloo</u>.
<u>When</u>? A raging fire destroyed the historic Colonial Inn in Waterloo <u>last night</u>.
<u>Why</u>? or <u>How</u>? A raging fire destroyed the historic Colonial Inn in Waterloo last night <u>after a bolt of lightning struck the building</u>.

Notice how the short sentence has been expanded to include more details. If you have a whole paragraph of short, choppy sentences, you can combine several of them by using any of the signal words listed in the box.

and	but	because	if	unless
or	for	when	after	while
yet	so	since	before	until

Assignment: Read the sentences below. Notice how some words are unnecessary or repeated. Try to combine all of the information in one or two sentences by using some of the signal words from the box above.

1. The monkey was at the Los Angeles Zoo.

2. The monkey lived in a large, open area.

3. The monkey's living area was surrounded by a wire fence.

4. The monkey's trainer fed him bananas and nuts.

5. The monkey liked to show off.

6. The monkey grinned and laughed at people who stopped to watch.

7. The monkey climbed large boulders.

8. The monkey swung on bars and poles.

_____

_____

_____

_____

_____

_____

REDUCING RUN-ON SENTENCES

Information: Run-on sentences are the result of overexpansion or combining too many ideas or phrases within one sentence. How can you avoid run-on sentences? Use the five suggestions listed below.

1. <u>Read your sentences orally</u>. If you pause, hesitate, or stop at certain points, you may need to insert a comma, semicolon, or period.

2. <u>Don't overuse connecting words</u>, such as "and," "when," "and then," "but," or "because." Limit the number of connecting words in each sentence.

3. <u>Watch for a change in subjects or ideas</u>. If the subject changes in the middle of a sentence, you may have a run-on sentence.

4. <u>Count the number of words per sentence</u>. If a sentence exceeds 20 words, check it carefully. Sentences of varying length improve the readability of a paragraph.

5. <u>Eliminate any unnecessary words or phrases</u>. Cross out extra words or repeated information.

Directions: Read the paragraph below with the five suggestions listed above in mind.

When my parents left me alone for the first time, I was excited about having the whole house to myself, but after a short time the sounds of the night made me uneasy because I never really noticed them before. Were the sounds normal or was there some creature or even worse a prowling thief who was trying to get into the house? First I decided to turn on all the lights and lock all the doors and windows and then I turned up the television's volume so that an intruder would know that someone was at home at this time. Watching the Alfred Hitchcock thriller *Psycho* on the television was a mistake because it made me even more aware of creaking floors, bushes scratching against the windowpane and Dr. George, our cat, jumping around upstairs. When the phone rang I jumped about three feet off the couch. It was my mother saying to me that Dad was not feeling well and that they were leaving and that they would be home in about 30 minutes. So much for staying home alone. I was relieved.

Assignment: Rewrite the paragraph, correcting the run-on sentences and eliminating as many unnecessary words as possible.

USING QUOTATION MARKS

Information: Quotation marks ("...") have several specialized uses, but usually they are used to enclose or surround the exact words someone has spoken or written. When writing dialogue in descriptive paragraphs, note the following major rules. An example is also given.

1. Use quotation marks to enclose every direct quote, whether it is complete or interrupted.

2. Both parts of an interrupted quotation are enclosed in quotation marks. The first word of the second part is *not* capitalized unless it begins a new sentence.

3. A change in speaker requires a new paragraph and a new set of quotation marks.

"May I use the car tonight?" Bill asked his father as he walked into the kitchen for dinner.
"Sure," replied Dad, "if you promise two things." Then he winked at Mom and continued. "You'll have to fill up the gas tank and agree to be home by 9 p.m."

Directions: Apply quotation marks and proper punctuation to the sentences below.

1. I deny everything you have said argued the accused shoplifter. But answered Sergeant Miller you were observed by our television camera taking those items.

2. When will you come home for Christmas vacation asked her mother. Will it be the 21st or the 22nd? I should be home the 21st replied Judy if Mr. Simpson gets here early enough I'll call you before we leave.

3. Mr. Williams said over the loudspeaker today's assembly has been postponed until further notice. In the teachers' room Miss Conable said I will now be able to give the vocabulary quiz to my third period class.

Assignment: Write a short descriptive dialogue (conversation) on one of the following topics:

1. teacher and student talking about a grade on a writing assignment.

2. David asking Sara for a date.

USING SIMILES AND METAPHORS

Information: Similes and metaphors are figures of speech that help to paint a clearer picture of what you are saying. They are used quite effectively in descriptive writing. Examples of these two figures of speech are given below.

Simile expresses a comparison, using "like" or "as."

Betty looks <u>like</u> an angel in that photo. (The subject "Betty" is compared to "an angel.")

Ralph is <u>as big as</u> a bear and wrestles like one, too. (The subject "Ralph" is compared to "a bear.")

Metaphor expresses a comparison in which readers use their imagination to see the likeness.

Betty is an angel in school. (The subject "Betty" is compared to "an angel.")

On the mat, Ralph is a bear. (The subject "Ralph" is compared to "a bear.")

Directions: Read the sentences below, which contain similes and metaphors. Underline the comparison and draw an arrow to its subject.

1. After a three-day absence, Rover ate like a starved pig.

2. On the gridiron, the Lions are the top of the heap.

3. They were a mass of nerves and tension after the accident.

4. He stood as still as a mannequin in a store window.

5. High in the sky the clouds were like puffs of cannon smoke.

6. His muscles turned hard as iron and he grew resistant to pain.

7. The first frost arrived unexpectedly and now the forests wear hoods of yellow and bronze.

8. In the west, the sun flared like a burning ball.

9. Muhammed Ali always proclaimed he could "float like a butterfly and sting like a bee."

10. I never liked school; it was merely a ticket to the employment agency.

11. Watching their 60-foot schooner point into the wind, I realized why she was called "the Grand Lady" of the sea.

12. The president of our student council is a stuffed shirt.

Assignment: Write six descriptive sentences of your own, three containing a simile and three with a metaphor.

APPEALING TO THE SENSES I

Information: When you write a descriptive paragraph you must first focus upon an image, which will be the topic. You can expand upon this image by using your senses to highlight the details. Hopefully, when you have finished, the reader will see, hear, taste, smell, or feel the image you chose to describe.

Directions: Read the paragraph below and answer the questions that follow.

As I walked into my English class for the first time this year, I wasn't expecting anything out of the ordinary. A few new faces in the class carried expressions of anxiety and nervousness. The others I'd seen for so many years hadn't changed at all. The odor of freshly painted walls and slippery, waxed floors indicated that the summer work crew had done its job. As usual, in Mr. Highland's room the desks and chairs were arranged in perfect rows. The chalkboards and bulletin boards were practically bare, with the exception of a new calendar and the regular assortment of mimeographed rules, regulations, and daily schedule. Just prior to the first period bell I heard whisperings that echoed my own thoughts, "Where's Mr. Highland? He's not at the board ready to squawk instructions—military style—at precisely 8:07." The low hum gradually increased in volume until 8:09 when the light scent of perfume rushed through the opening door. Silence. In walked a pretty, long-haired woman, stylishly dressed and obviously new. With a smile that caught everyone's eye, she gently said, "Good morning. My name is Miss Thompson. I've replaced the retired Mr. Highland." This might be an interesting year after all!

1. What is the topic? _____

2. How does the writer feel about the topic? _____

_____

3. To which senses does the writer appeal? _____

_____

4. Write the words or phrases from the paragraph that convey each sense impression.

Sight: _____

_____

Hearing: _____

_____

Taste: _____

_____

Touch: _____

_____

Smell: _____

_____

Assignment: Write a descriptive paragraph about your first class this year.

APPEALING TO THE SENSES II: SIGHT

Information: Describing is really an easy task when you use your sense of sight. You can describe objects, activities, events, or people much more accurately in this way. What is your topic's color, size, or shape? What special features does it have? Is it in motion or stationary? What can you say about its surroundings? Sometimes the topic is visible while you are writing. In most cases, however, you must rely on past experience to help you visualize the topic. Follow the two steps listed below *before* you begin writing.

1. Focus on the topic—either through memory or through observation.

2. Write down any words or phrases that describe how your topic *looks*.

Directions: Read the topic below and the visual details that follow. Think about how you would organize those details as you prepare to write a paragraph about the topic.

Huge Christmas tree in department store.

Glittering ornaments reflecting light; many sizes and shapes of wrapped presents; at least 25 feet high with flashing star at the top; silvery tinsel hanging; green felt rope connected to four heavy stands; flickering red, yellow, green, blue lights; strings of popcorn draped around; first sight upon entering front door; smiling shoppers staring.

Assignment: Write a paragraph using any of the listed details (and any others you want to add) to describe the topic.

_____

_____

_____

_____

_____

_____

_____

_____

_____

_____

_____

_____

APPEALING TO THE SENSES III: HEARING

Information: Appealing to the sense of hearing also helps to paint a clear picture of your topic. Listen to or try to remember all the sounds related to the object, activity, event, or person. Are the sounds loud, soft, or rhythmic? Do they blend well together or compete with each other for your attention? Does the noise you hear come directly from the object or is it part of the background? Answering these questions will help you to describe your topic more clearly and accurately. Follow the two steps below *before* you begin writing.

  1. Focus on the topic—either through memory or through observation.

  2. Write down any words or phrases that describe the *sounds* of or around your topic.

Directions: Read the topic below and the details that follow. Think about how you would organize those details as you prepare to write a paragraph about the topic.

Department store during Christmas holiday season.

Television programs and stereo equipment blaring; cash registers ringing; crinkling of customers' shopping bags; clerks explaining products; holiday music playing softly through hidden speakers; teenagers testing latest electronic games with computerized voices and sirens; ringing bells; the roaring "Ho, ho, ho!" of Santa Claus; crying babies; young boys and girls squealing over games and toys they want.

Assignment: Write a paragraph using any of the listed details (and any others you want to add) to describe the topic.

_____

_____

_____

_____

_____

_____

_____

_____

_____

_____

_____

_____

_____

APPEALING TO THE SENSES IV: TOUCH, TASTE, AND SMELL

Information: The senses of touch, taste, and smell appeal to the reader very effectively. We are all naturally attracted to things that evoke them, and companies who advertise their products on radio and television use this technique to their advantage. Expressions like "cold and tingling," "downy soft," and "like a breath of fresh air" are used to attract our attention and create feelings of comfort and satisfaction. Try to create your own impression by appealing to the senses of touch, taste, and smell. Follow the two steps listed below *before* you begin writing.

1. Focus on the topic—either through memory or through observation.

2. Write down any words or phrases that appeal to *touch, taste,* and *smell.*

Directions: Read the topic below and the details that follow. Think about how you would organize those details as you prepare to write a paragraph about the topic.

Department store during Christmas holiday season.

Fluffy down quilt; scratchy sweater; cheese and cracker samples; roasted peanuts and buttery popcorn; bayberry- and vanilla-scented candles; rolling and swaying on displayed waterbed; popular fragrances from perfume and cologne counter; over-carbonated soft drink; sizzling hot cheeseburger; greasy French fries.

Assignment: Write a paragraph using any of the listed details (and any others you want to add) to describe the topic.

_____

_____

_____

_____

_____

_____

_____

_____

_____

_____

_____

_____

_____

_____

APPEALING TO THE SENSES V: COMBINING SENSES

Information: You have learned how each of the senses of sight, hearing, taste, touch, and smell can be used individually to effectively describe your topic. In reality, it might be difficult to write a paragraph that appeals to only one sense. Therefore, you should try to use a combination of two or more.

Directions: Read the following paragraph. Note how the senses are combined to form an effective picture.

As I trotted into McGuire's Department Store to buy some Christmas gifts, I was shocked by the size and beauty of their Christmas tree. Flickering red, yellow, green, and blue lights reflected off the hundreds of glittering ornaments. From the assortment of colorfully wrapped packages at its base to the glowing star on its top, that 25-foot blue spruce was a masterpiece of decoration. I was not the only one impressed by this display. Nearly everyone stopped to stare before continuing on his or her way. The piped-in holiday music was occasionally drowned out by the blaring stereo equipment, crying babies, or the electronic games with their computerized voices and sirens. But they all created a festive mood. On my way to the Junior Miss Department, I sampled the latest fragrances at the perfume counter and rolled on the displayed waterbed. I wanted to buy a sweater for my sister, but the ones I could afford were too scratchy. Instead, I bought her a bayberry-scented candle shaped like a unicorn. As I wandered about from department to department, the smell of roasted peanuts and buttery popcorn drew me to the restaurant counter. That was a mistake. The over-carbonated soda had too much syrup and the French fries were greasy. On top of that, the sizzling cheeseburger burned the roof of my mouth. On my way out, the ringing cash registers and overstuffed shopping bags indicated that customers were in a buying mood. I suddenly realized that I had a lot more shopping to do.

Assignment: List the words in the above paragraph that appeal to the five senses.

Sight

Hearing

Taste

Touch

Smell

APPEALING TO THE SENSES VI: APPLICATION

Directions: Below are two topics that you could describe very colorfully by appealing to the senses. Select one and jot down details for each sense that could describe the scene. Then write two or three possible introductions and select the best one.

  1. A busy city street corner.

  2. A cafeteria in school or a restaurant.

Sight details _____

_____

Hearing details _____

_____

Touch details _____

_____

Taste details _____

_____

Smell details _____

_____

Introduction #1 _____

_____

_____

Introduction #2 _____

_____

_____

Introduction #3 _____

_____

_____

Which introduction is the best? _____

Assignment: Write a paragraph or paragraphs describing your topic in detail. Be sure to appeal to as many senses as possible.

DESCRIBING A PERSON I

Information: Describing a person is far different from describing an object, event, or activity. You must try to capture both the physical features and the personality traits of an individual. Does his appearance tell you something about his personality? How does he act with other individuals, in small groups, or in large gatherings? What mannerisms make him different from others? How does he walk, talk, or dress? If done well, your description will identify the person without mentioning the name.

Directions: Read the paragraph below and answer the questions that follow.

When he walks into the room you can sense the seriousness with which he performs his job. A long nose and high cheekbones dwarf the rest of his face. Black-rimmed glasses cannot hide those dark, penetrating eyes that immediately photograph all activity in the room. Meticulously dressed in a pinstriped suit and wrinkle-free, button-down shirt, he is a perfectionist. Everything and every person has its place; order and organization are the rule. He walks and stands erect, looking much like a military officer who has arrived for inspection. With a quick glance and a forced smile, he turns and walks away. He conveys his message clearly without uttering a single word. The clicking of those spit-shined shoes echoes through the halls as he makes his way back to the principal's office.

1. What are the words that describe what he looks like? _____

_____

_____

_____

2. Which words describe his personality traits? _____

_____

_____

_____

3. How does the author feel about him? _____

_____

_____

4. Why do you think so? _____

_____

5. What is your impression of him? _____

_____

_____

_____

DESCRIBING A PERSON II

Information: When describing a person you must try to capture both her physical characteristics and personality traits. Describe how she acts alone or with others. What does she do with her hands, eyes, and body? What does she say and how does she say it? How does her appearance or dress relate to her personality? Answering these questions might help you describe a person more effectively.

Directions: Describe a person in your class so that others will be able to identify him or her. Follow these rules:

1. Do not tell anyone else whom you are describing.

2. Do not refer to that person as "him," "her," or by name.

3. Do not describe out-of-class behavior.

Assignment: Write the description below. Appeal to the senses and organize the description in an orderly manner, such as from head to toe or from side to side.

_____

_____

_____

_____

_____

_____

_____

_____

_____

_____

_____

_____

_____

_____

_____

_____

_____

ORGANIZING PARAGRAPHS

Information: There are several ways to organize descriptive paragraphs. The details, especially in sight description, should follow a logical sequence. You may describe your scene from side to side, from near to far (or reverse), or from top to bottom (or reverse). The following list of signal words may guide you in developing this organization.

base	across	interior	upward	at a distance
bottom	below	exterior	within	to (on) the left
foot	beneath	next to	close	to (on) the right
top	center	under	against	in back of
above	middle	underneath	near	in front of
behind	peak	crest	summit	leading to
beside	halfway	up	down	far

Directions: Read the paragraph below and answer the questions that follow.

I was late for the football game, but at least my car was now running properly. As I pulled into the parking lot, I could see the scoreboard at a distance. With two minutes remaining in the second quarter, the score read "Eagles 0, Visitors 0." I guessed that I hadn't missed too much. I walked through the gate leading to the stadium. The closer I got to the playing field, the more the excitement mounted. I hurried across the end zone and noticed that the Eagles were in a position to score at the far end of the field. Looking for my friends in Section B was difficult as the bodies and faces blurred together. Suddenly there was a roar, and everyone jumped up and down in a frenzy. The Eagles had scored. I stood at the base of the stands waiting for the crowd to settle down. Finally I spotted Dick and Phil about halfway up. Their faces reflected the joy and excitement of all Eagle fans as the gun sounded, ending the first half.

1. What method of organization is used? _____

_____

2. What words signal this method? _____

_____

_____

Assignment: Write a paragraph describing a scene, activity, or person. Use the signal words to help you organize the information.

ORGANIZING BY POSITION: PREPOSITIONAL PHRASES

Information: One way to improve your descriptive writing is to identify the position or location of your subject as clearly as possible. You can do this by using prepositional phrases. Look at the list of prepositions in the box below.

aboard	behind	from	to
about	below	in	toward
above	beneath	into	under
across	beside	next to	underneath
against	between	of	up
along	beyond	off	upon
among	by	on	with
around	down	over	within
at	for	through	without

Directions: Read the story below, placing reasonable prepositions in the blanks. Notice that the story is much more exact when you use prepositional phrases that identify location and position.

No one had ever escaped _____ Thunder Island! Major Martin planned his escape as soon as he arrived _____ this devilish island. At first he was thrown _____ the dungeon _____ ground level. It was dank and dark as he felt his way _____ the cell he was to call home _____ the next ten years. Immediately he knew that the best way out was to tunnel _____ the stone foundation, _____ the 1,500-foot prisoner yard, and _____ the snake-infested swamp. Then he could attempt to find his way _____ the sea and freedom.

Digging _____ his fingers and a flat stone that he found _____ his bed, Major Martin managed to work his way _____ the hard-packed sand for the first 50 feet _____ his journey _____ liberty. As he moved slowly _____ the torture chamber, he could hear screaming.

Assignment: Complete this story, using prepositional phrases that accurately describe position or location.

ORGANIZING WITH TIME SIGNALS

Information: A writer o ten uses signal words to help his readers understand how the ideas in the paragraph are related to each other in time. The words in the box below can be used to show how events are related by time order or sequence.

first	then	before . . .
second	immediately	soon
next	meanwhile	before long
at the same time	thereafter	finally
later	afterwards	at last
after . . .	earlier	

Notice how some of these signal words are used in the following paragraph:

The weather was very changeable today. <u>First</u>, the sun shone so brightly I needed sunglasses. <u>Then</u> gray storm clouds rolled in from the west. <u>After lunch</u>, lightning darted across the sky and the thunder sent my chickens running for cover. <u>Before long</u>, huge, cold raindrops fell in a torrent. <u>Later that afternoon</u>, the rain stopped, the clouds disappeared, and the blue sky <u>finally</u> reappeared.

As you can see, the underlined signal words help to identify the order in which things are happening. These signal words can be especially useful when writing a summary, a book report, or a story.

Assignment: Write your own story, using the introductory sentence below. Be sure to use the signal words whenever possible.

"That one day as an invisible person was really an unbelievable experience for me!"

ORGANIZING BY CAUSE AND EFFECT

Information: Certain events or activities can lead to *(cause)* another event *(effect)*. You can use this cause and effect pattern very effectively when writing descriptive paragraphs. The signal words listed in the box below may help you to organize your paragraph in a cause-and-effect pattern.

since	because	thus	caused by
due to	therefore	so	as a result of
because of	consequently	if—then	for this reason
whenever	when		

Directions: Read the paragraph below. Look for the signal words or phrases that indicate when one event may cause something else to happen. Then answer the questions that follow.

It was one of those hot, sticky, stormy nights when even the soundest sleepers would be lucky to get more than three hours of sleep. A heavy vapor hung over the city like a soaked blanket; the result of a late afternoon thunder shower. The temperature registered 81° at 10 p.m., and I'm sure the humidity was 100%. Consequently, my sweat-covered body could not find a comfortable spot in which to relax, much less fall asleep. I could tell another storm was brewing when flashes of lightning in the distance disrupted the 11 o'clock radio newscast. I must have fallen asleep for a short time when all at once a crack of thunder shook my apartment and caused me to sit up in bed instantly. I could hear the gusts of wind and driving rain beating against my window. As I lay sleeplessly on my bed, it seemed the storm would never end. Suddenly I realized it was daylight, and my heart jumped when I looked at the clock. It read 2:59. Obviously the storm had caused a power blackout. Racing around the apartment, I hoped I would not be late for work.

1. List the words or phrases that signal causes or effects in this paragraph.

_____

_____

_____

2. What are some of the causes and effects used in this paragraph? _____

_____

_____

_____

Assignment: Choose one of the three topics listed below or one of your own and write a descriptive paragraph using the cause-and-effect pattern of organization. Use the signal words when necessary.

1. A traffic accident you observed.

2. An argument between two students.

3. A party you attended.

ORGANIZING IDEAS BY USING DETAILS I

Information: One way to organize ideas in descriptive writing is to brainstorm for words or phrases that come to mind when you think of a particular topic. Then organize those random thoughts according to a plan. You could describe your topic from outside to inside, from top to bottom, from one spot to another, or from far to near. Remember to start your paragraphs with a general statement about the topic.

Directions: Read the topic below and the details that follow. Think about how you would organize those details as you prepare to write a paragraph about the topic.

An old barn in the country.

Weather-worn; dull red with faded white letters advertising Mail Pouch Tobacco; haven for field mice and farm cats; pigeons perched on huge 12-inch beams; burdocks and grape vines crawling up sides; standing idle for many years; alongside country road; notice every time I drive by; old stone foundation crumbling; door blown off; rough to the touch; could see daylight through holes in the siding and roof.

Assignment: Write a paragraph using the details listed above (and any others you want to add). Remember to organize the ideas according to a plan and to write a good topic sentence.

_____

_____

_____

_____

_____

_____

_____

_____

_____

_____

_____

_____

_____

ORGANIZING IDEAS BY USING DETAILS II

Directions: Choose one of the following topics and try to visualize or imagine in detail what it looks like, sounds like, smells like, or even feels like. What does it remind you of? What can you compare it to? How do you feel about it? Write down these thoughts quickly; they do not have to be in any particular order. Then decide how you will organize the details.

Topics

1. Christmas or birthday morning.
2. a burned-out building.
3. a messy bedroom.
4. your first day of school.
5. a county or state fair.
6. your choice of any other topic.

Details

———————————————————————————————————

———————————————————————————————————

———————————————————————————————————

———————————————————————————————————

———————————————————————————————————

———————————————————————————————————

———————————————————————————————————

———————————————————————————————————

———————————————————————————————————

———————————————————————————————————

———————————————————————————————————

———————————————————————————————————

How will you organize these details?———————————————————

———————————————————————————————————

Assignment: Write a descriptive paragraph using the details listed above. Remember to organize the ideas according to a plan and to write a good topic sentence.

REVISING I: MECHANICS

Information: When you write the first draft of your descriptive paragraph, you are probably interested primarily in organizing the details into sentences and paragraphs. It is only natural to make errors in spelling, capitalization, punctuation, grammar, and usage. It is important to read through these first drafts carefully looking for any errors. Many writers read them orally to see if they "sound" right.

Directions: Read the following paragraph and look for any mechanical errors.

I enjoy living in a big old house in the country even though it is sandwiched in between a State Highway and the railroad tracks. Standing in front of this solidly built brick structure you can tell it is more than 100 years old and can imagine it will stand straight and square for another century. Once inside I don't really notice the heavy highway traffic the thick brick walls and overgrown forsythia bushes help to deaden the sound of tractor trailers and speeding cars. I especially like the inside of my house and its special features wide plank floors natural chestnut woodwork four working fireplaces and a huge eat-in kitchen. Everyone has their own bedroom in a large house and I can always find privacy in my roon. The railroad tracks are not visible as you walk out the back door. A row of poplar trees and evergreens sheild the view. Yes the trains are noisy when they pass, but after 16 years in this house, I don't even remember how often it goes by. Some people may prefer living in a city apartment or a quieter country road, but I could live in my house forever.

Check any areas below that might be problems in the paragraph. Be prepared to support your answers.

_____Spelling   _____Capitalization   _____Other

_____Grammar/Usage   _____Punctuation

Assignment: Revise and rewrite the paragraph. Eliminate any errors in mechanics.

_____

_____

_____

_____

_____

_____

REVISING II: EDITING

Information: Most writers are well aware of the need to make revisions of their first draft in the areas of spelling, punctuation, grammar, and usage. However, it is also important to check for other problems. Do you have an eye-catching introduction that previews the rest of the paragraph? Is your paragraph organized? You should not have repeated yourself or included information that is unrelated to the topic. Be sure to reread your first draft and look for any editorial errors.

Directions: Read the paragraph below and answer the questions that follow.

Thanksgiving Day is one of my favorite holidays because the whole family gets together for a day of playing, talking, and feasting. Waiting until the traditional 3 p.m. serving time is agonizing. Just before sitting down to eat, I marvel at my mother's colorful display of food. It looks like a photograph from *Cuisine* Magazine: green leafy vegetables and salads, yellow squash and corn, golden brown turkey and duckling ready for my father's carving knife, crimson red beets and cranberry sauce, fluffy potatoes and stuffing, and deep, rich gravy. From the moment I wake I hear the clanging of pots and pans as well as the familiar hum of the dishwasher. It makes no difference what the weather is like outside because we stay inside most of the day. The smells of butterbasted turkey, fresh-baked rolls, and creamy pumpkin pies fill our house all day long. Even though breakfast and lunch are not served, we can snack on fresh fruits and vegetables, cheese, crackers, and nuts while patiently waiting for the main course. Despite our hunger, there is always more than enough food to feed this family of ten. Completely stuffed, my twin brother and I retire to our room to watch football games on television. I have the feeling I may never eat again, at least until early evening.

1. Is the introduction a general statement about the rest of the paragraph? _____ Why or why not? _____

_____

2. Are the details organized in a logical way? _____ If not, how could they be arranged? _____

_____

3. Do all the details relate to the introduction? _____ If not, which ones would you eliminate? _____

_____

4. Has any of the information been repeated? _____ If so, what could be eliminated? _____

_____

Assignment: Revise and rewrite the paragraph to eliminate any problems that exist.

_____

_____

_____

_____

_____

REVISING III: WORD CHOICE

Information: When you write the final draft of your descriptive paragraph, your main concern is in getting the ideas and organization on paper. Therefore, you do not always think of the best word or phrase to use at that time. Sometimes you put a word or phrase in the wrong place. Other times you may overuse a word or phrase. While reading over your first draft, substitute active verbs for inactive ones, replace overused or vague nouns with more precise ones, and try to eliminate unnecessary words or phrases.

Directions: Read the descriptive paragraph below. Circle any words that are overused. Cross out unnecessary words. Underline those words that could be expressed more accurately.

The most memorable part of the ferry ride to the Massachusetts island of Martha's Vineyard was watching the seagulls follow the boat. I was thoroughly entertained by watching several passengers tempt the birds with pieces of bread. They held their arms over the side of the boat and waited for the birds to take the bread out of their hands. Eight or ten birds hovered above the deck, waiting for the right moment to fly down and take the bread from the passengers' hands. I was impressed with how the birds rode the air currents, coasting effortlessly up and down and around. I was surprised at how quickly this 45-minute trip passed and I was determined to bring some bread of my own for the return trip.

Assignment: Revise and rewrite the paragraph by using more accurate and precise words.

PRACTICE AND REVIEW I

Directions: Choose one of the topics below or use one of your own. In the spaces provided list any details that appeal to the senses. Next, write two different introductions, or leads, for your topic. Choose the better introduction and decide how to organize the notes.

1. A person in your class.

2. A trip into outer space.

3. Your first visit to the dentist.

Sight details _____

_____

Hearing details _____

_____

Touch details _____

_____

Taste details _____

_____

Smell details _____

_____

Introduction #1 _____

_____

_____

Introduction #2 _____

_____

_____

Type of organization _____

_____

Assignment: Write your first draft by organizing the notes above. Then write a descriptive paragraph (or paragraphs) about your topic. Remember to revise the first draft before writing the paragraph.

PRACTICE AND REVIEW II

Directions: Choose one of the topics below or use one of your own. In the spaces provided, list any details that appeal to the senses. Next, write two different introductions, or leads, for your topic. Choose the better introduction and decide how to organize the notes.

1. A haunted house.

2. A sidewalk sale.

3. A brother, sister, or other family member.

Sight details _____

_____

Hearing details _____

_____

Touch details _____

_____

Taste details _____

_____

Smell details _____

_____

Introduction #1 _____

_____

_____

Introduction #2 _____

_____

_____

Type of organization _____

_____

Assignment: Write your first draft by organizing the notes above. Then write a descriptive paragraph (or paragraphs) about your topic. Remember to revise the first draft before writing the paragraph.

PRACTICE AND REVIEW III

Directions: Choose one of the topics below or use one of your own. In the spaces provided list any details that appeal to the senses. Next, write two different introductions, or leads, for your topic. Choose the better introduction and decide how to organize the notes.

1. A state, county, or town fair.

2. A rock concert.

3. Your favorite pastime or hobby.

Sight details _____

_____

Hearing details _____

_____

Touch details _____

_____

Taste details _____

_____

Smell details _____

_____

Introduction #1 _____

_____

_____

Introduction #2 _____

_____

_____

Type of organization _____

_____

Assignment: Write your first draft by organizing the notes above. Then write a descriptive paragraph (or paragraphs) about your topic. Remember to revise the first draft before writing the paragraph.

PRACTICE AND REVIEW IV

Directions: Choose one of the topics below or use one of your own. In the spaces provided, list any details that appeal to the senses. Next, write two different introductions, or leads, for your topic. Choose the better introduction and decide how to organize the notes.

1. A fall (winter, spring, summer) day.
2. An amusement park.
3. Your best friend.

Sight details _____

_____

Hearing details _____

_____

Touch details _____

_____

Taste details _____

_____

Smell details _____

_____

Introduction #1 _____

_____

_____

Introduction #2 _____

_____

_____

Type of organization _____

_____

Assignment: Write your first draft by organizing the notes above. Then write a descriptive paragraph (or paragraphs) about your topic. Remember to revise the first draft before writing the paragraph.

PRACTICE AND REVIEW V

Directions: Choose one of the topics below or use one of your own. In the spaces provided, list any details that appeal to the senses. Next, write two different introductions, or leads, for your topic. Choose the better introduction and decide how to organize the notes.

1. A restaurant you like.

2. An athletic contest or event.

3. What you would do if you won the lottery.

Sight details _____

_____

Hearing details _____

_____

Touch details _____

_____

Taste details _____

_____

Smell details _____

_____

Introduction #1 _____

_____

_____

Introduction #2 _____

_____

_____

Type of organization _____

_____

Assignment: Write your first draft by organizing the notes above. Then write a descriptive paragraph (or paragraphs) about your topic. Remember to revise the first draft before writing the paragraph.

DESCRIPTIVE WRITING: OUTLINE FORM

Topic _____

Sight details _____

_____

_____

Hearing details _____

_____

_____

Touch details _____

_____

_____

Taste details _____

_____

_____

Smell details _____

_____

_____

Introduction (lead) #1 _____

_____

_____

Introduction (lead) #2 _____

_____

_____

Conclusion _____

_____

_____

Type of organization _____
                   (position, time order, cause/effect)

DW 34

DESCRIPTIVE WRITING TOPICS

1. Write about any spontaneous incidents.

2. Write about any pictures, photos, or objects.

3. Write about the person next to (beside, in front of) you.

4. Write a fable, such as "The Frog and the Waterfly."

5. Blindfold yourself and describe how something feels, tastes, smells, and sounds.

6. Without using any proper nouns, describe how to get from _____ (school, the post office) to _____ (home, the park).

7. "My trip to _____ was just incredible."

8. "As I woke up and came to my senses, I realized that I could not see."

9. "When I stepped around the corner onto Main Street, I could not believe what I was seeing."

10. "My life as a(n) _____ proved to be extremely dangerous."

11. "Our last camping trip was the most _____ weekend of my life."

12. "My life as a _____ (mouse, snake) was _____ ."

DESCRIPTIVE WRITING: SIGNAL WORDS

Connective

after	since
and	so
because	unless
before	until
but	when
for	while
if	yet
or	

Prepositions

aboard	behind	from	to
about	below	in	toward
above	beneath	into	under
across	beside	next to	underneath
against	between	of	up
along	beyond	off	upon
among	by	on	with
around	down	over	within
at	for	through	without

Time Order

after ...	earlier	next
afterwards	finally	second
at least	first	soon
at the same time	immediately	then
before ...	later	thereafter
before long	meanwhile	

Cause and Effect

as a result of	if—then
because	since
because of	so
caused by	therefore
consequently	thus
due to	when
for this reason	whenever

Position

above	crest	next to
across	down	peak
against	exterior	summit
at a distance	far	to (on) the left
base	foot	to (on) the right
behind	halfway	top
below	in back of	under
beneath	in front of	underneath
beside	interior	up
bottom	leading to	upward
close	near	

ANSWER KEY

DW 1

1. Miss Jackson thought I was a troublemaker.
2. yes.
3. no.
4. One time I convinced a friend of mine to go to the office without Miss Jackson's knowledge.

He got in trouble but never told on me.

I'm sure she sensed that I was not so interested in schoolwork as I was in recess or gym because I always came to school with athletic equipment of some sort.

My sixth-grade teacher, Miss Jackson, thought I was a troublemaker and I can only guess the reasons why. Maybe it was because I enjoyed laughing and playing practical jokes on my friends. Since I was big for my age and my voice began to change, Miss Jackson probably felt I had repeated a grade or two. Therefore, I must have been a troublemaker in her eyes. Furthermore, a student always knows when the teacher doesn't trust him or her. Those eagle-eye stares and the pacing behind my desk were warnings enough of the distrust. I guess I'll never know the real reasons, but there's no doubt she thought I was a troublemaker.

DW 2

1. Accept any answer with a reasonable explanation.
2. Accept any answer with a reasonable explanation.

Assignment: Answers will vary. Each lead should be slightly different and students should offer a reasonable explanation for selecting their "best" lead.

DW 3

Answers will vary. Samples:
3. He turned out to be my best friend.
4. After I really got to know a few people, it was just like I had been there for years.
5. I learned to appreciate the beauty of nature.
6. It is convenient transportation, but not very enjoyable.

Assignment: Answers will vary. Emphasis should be placed on a logical plotting of information leading to the conclusion.

DW 4

Answers will vary. Sample:
Descriptive adjectives in blanks: Oakridge, most terrifying, tree-lined, grocery, nickel, cold, iron, cozy, ghost, mysterious, chilling, clear, balmy, dark, cold, horrible, comic, whining, faint, stone, huckleberry, strange, oddly shaped.

Assignment: Answers will vary. Be sure students emphasize their use of adjectives.

DW 5

Answers will vary. Samples:
Directions:
1. nail-biting, hilarious.
2. meticulous, friendly.
3. shocking, unforgettable.
4. delicious, scrumptious.
5. average, conscientious.
Practice:
1. lonely, satisfying.
2. unpopular, shy.
3. little, hardy.
4. valuable, life-long.
5. enclosed, two-room.
6. organized, systematic.

Assignment: Answers will vary. Be sure students avoid the use of vague adjectives, such as "good," "great," "pretty."

DW 6

Answers will vary. Sample:
Action-packed verbs: teach, in the end, received, acquired, complained, relented, whispered, annoyed, pounded, pranced, devised, buy.
Assignment: Answers will vary. Students should avoid inactive or passive verbs.

DW 7

Answers will vary. Sample:
Descriptive adverbs: vividly, nervously, always, eagerly, Later, loudly, wildly, hungrily.
Assignment: Answers will vary. Students should emphasize their use of descriptive adverbs.

DW 8

Answers will vary. Sample:
   The monkey lived in a large, open area surrounded by a wire fence at the Los Angeles Zoo, and he liked to show off after his trainer fed him bananas and nuts. When people

stopped to watch, he grinned and laughed, swung on bars and poles, or climbed large boulders.

DW 9

When my parents left me alone for the first time, I was excited about having the whole house to myself. But after a short time, the sounds of the night made me uneasy because I never really noticed them before. Were the sounds normal? Was there some creature or a prowling thief trying to get in the house? First, I decided to turn on all the lights and lock all the doors and windows. Then I turned up the television's volume so an intruder would know that someone was home. Watching the Alfred Hitchcock thriller *Psycho* on the television was a mistake. It made me even more aware of creaking floors, bushes scratching against the windowpane, and Dr. George, our cat, jumping around upstairs. When the phone rang I jumped about three feet off the couch. It was my mother saying Dad was ill, so they were leaving the dinner and would be home in thirty minutes. So much for staying home alone. I was relieved.

DW 10

1.   "I deny everything you have said," argued the accused shoplifter.
        "But," answered Sergeant Miller, "you were observed by our television camera taking those items."
2.   "When will you come home for Christmas vacation?" asked her mother. "Will it be the twenty-first or the twenty-second?"
        "I should be home the twenty-first," replied Judy. "If Mr. Simpson gets here early enough, I'll call you before we leave."
3.   Mr. Williams said over the loudspeaker, "Today's assembly has been postponed until further notice."
        In the teachers' room Miss Conable said, "I will now be able to give the vocabulary quiz to my third period class."

Assignment: Answers will vary. Students should correctly place punctuation and quotation marks.

DW 11

1. Comparison: a starved pig. Subject: Rover.
2. Comparison: the top of the heap. Subject: Lions.
3. Comparison: a mass of nerves and tension. Subject: They.
4. Comparison: a mannequin. Subject: He.
5. Comparison: puffs of cannon smoke. Subject: clouds.
6. Comparison: hard as iron. Subject: muscles.
7. Comparison: hoods of yellow and bronze. Subject: forests.
8. Comparison: a burning ball. Subject: sun.
9. Comparison: a butterfly and a bee. Subject: Muhammed Ali.

10. Comparison: a ticket. Subject: school.
11. Comparison: the Grand Lady of the sea. Subject: schooner.
12. Comparison: a stuffed shirt. Subject: student council president.

Assignment: Answers will vary. Be sure students use similes and metaphors correctly.

DW 12

1. Reactions to first English class.
2. A bit apprehensive at first; then excited about the new teacher.
3. sight, hearing, touch, smell.
4. *Sight:*   faces carried expressions of anxiety and nervousness
            no changes in others
            desks and chairs arranged in perfect rows
            chalkboards and bulletin boards practically bare
            new calendar and the regular assortment of mimeographed rules, regulations,
               and daily schedule
            pretty, long-haired woman, stylishly dressed
            a smile that caught everyone's eye
   Hearing: heard whisperings
            squawk instructions
            low hum
            Silence
            gently said
   Taste: (none)
   Touch: slippery waxed floors
   Smell: odor of freshly painted walls
            light scent of perfume

Assignment: Answers will vary. Students should include as many sensory images as possible.

DW 13

Answers will vary. See model paragraph on activity page DW 16 for sample.

DW 14

Answers will vary. See model paragraph on activity page DW 16 for sample.

DW 15

Answers will vary. See model paragraph on activity page DW 16 for sample.

DW 16

Sight: size and beauty of Christmas tree
flickering red, yellow, green, blue lights
glittering ornaments
colorfully wrapped packages
glowing star on top
shaped like a unicorn
overstuffed shopping bags
Hearing: piped-in holiday music
blaring stereo equipment
crying babies
electronic games with computerized voices and sirens
ringing cash registers
Taste: over-carbonated soda
greasy French fries
sizzling cheeseburger
Touch: rolled on waterbed
scratchy sweaters
burned roof of mouth
Smell: latest fragrances at perfume counter
bayberry-scented candle
roasted peanuts and buttery popcorn

DW 17

Answers will vary. Students should include as many sensory details as possible and attempt to write at least two different introductions.

DW 18

1. long nose; high cheekbones; black-rimmed glasses; dark, penetrating eyes; pinstriped suit; wrinkle-free, button-down shirt; spit-shined shoes.
2. seriousness; meticulously dressed; perfectionist; orderly and organized; walks and stands erect.

Answers will vary. Samples:
3. The author doesn't like him very much, but respects his authority.
4. The author compares him to a military officer. He doesn't say anything, just stares and forces a smile.
5. He's all business and not very friendly. He demands respect and probably gets it.

DW 19

Answers will vary. Students should include several sensory images in a logical organization.

DW 20

1. far to near.
2. at a distance, The closer I got, at the far end of the field, at the base of the stands.

Assignment: Answers will vary. Students should emphasize the positional organization of the paragraph.

DW 21

Answers will vary. Samples:
Prepositions in blanks: from, at, into, below, through, for, beneath, under, around, toward, with, beside, through, of, to, by.
Assignment: Answers will vary. Students should describe position or location by using prepositional phrases.

DW 22

Answers will vary. Students should use time signals.

DW 23

1. when, the result of, Consequently, when, when, caused, when, caused.
2. hot, sticky night caused sleeplessness; thunderstorm resulted in heavy vapor; humidity caused body to sweat; sweaty body could not get comfortable; flashes of lightning interrupted news; thunder woke me up; storm caused a blackout.

Assignment: Answers will vary. Students should show evidence of cause and effect patterns and use corresponding signal words.

DW 24

Answers will vary. Sample:

Have you ever noticed that old weather-worn barn that sits close to the road on Dublin Lane? Since it has been standing idle for a long time, I decided to stop one day and take a closer look. Its dull red color still outlined and faded white letters advertising Mail Pouch Tobacco. As I got closer, I saw burdocks embedded in the crumbling stone foundation and grape vines were crawling up the rough-edged siding. I stepped through an unprotected entrance, catching a glimpse of an old door that had obviously blown off several years ago. Once inside the barn, I could see daylight peeping through holes in the siding and roof. A dozen or more pigeons were perched on huge 12-inch beams, but flapped their wings and shifted positions in response to my intrusion. I thought this must be a haven for field mice, because a scrawny barn cat was bounding about a hay pile toying with this morning's catch. On the way back to the car, I kept wondering who owned this decrepit barn and why it was no longer used.

DW 25

Answers will vary. Students should list sensory images and comparisons, and organize the details by position, time order, or cause and effect.

DW 26

Areas checked: spelling, grammar/usage, capitalization, punctuation, other.

I enjoy living in a big old house in the country, even though it is sandwiched between a state highway and the railroad tracks. Standing in front of this solidly built brick structure, I can tell it is more than 100 years old. I imagine it will be straight and square for another century. Once inside, I don't really notice the heavy highway traffic because the thick brick walls and overgrown forsythia bushes deaden the sound of tractor trailers and speeding cars. I especially like the inside of my house and its special features: wide plank floors, natural chestnut woodwork, four working fireplaces, and a huge eat-in kitchen. Everyone has his or her own bedroom in a large house and I can always find privacy in my room. The railroad tracks are not visible as you walk out the back door. A row of poplar trees and evergreens shield the view. Yes, the trains are noisy when they pass, but after 16 years in this house, I don't even remember how often they pass. Some people may prefer living in a city apartment or on a quieter country road, but I could live in my house forever.

DW 27

1. no. There is no discussion of playing or talking in the paragraph.
2. no. Details can be arranged in time order.
3. no. "It makes no difference what the weather is like outside because we stay inside most of the day."
4. no.

Answers will vary. Sample:

Thanksgiving Day is one of my favorite holidays because the whole family gets together in anticipation of a great feast. However, waiting until the traditional 3 p.m. serving time is agonizing. From the moment I wake, I hear the clanging of pots and pans and the familiar hum of the dishwasher. The smells of butterbasted turkey, fresh-baked rolls and creamy pumpkin pies fill our house all day long. Even though breakfast and lunch are not served, we can snack on fresh fruits and vegetables, cheese, crackers, and nuts while waiting patiently for the main course. Just before sitting down to eat, I marvel at my mother's colorful display of food. It looks like a photograph from *Cuisine* magazine: green, leafy vegetables and salads, yellow squash and corn, golden brown turkey and duckling for my father's carving knife, crimson red beets and cranberry sauce, fluffy potatoes and stuffing, and deep, rich gravy. Despite our hunger, there is always more than enough food for this family of ten. Completely stuffed, my twin brother and I retire to our room to watch football games on television. I have the feeling I may never eat again, at least until early evening!

DW 28

Answers will vary. Sample:

  The most memorable part of the ferry ride to the Massachusetts island of Martha's Vineyard was watching the seagulls follow the boat. I was thoroughly entertained while several passengers tempted the gulls with pieces of bread. They held their arms over the side of the boat and baited the birds. Eight or ten seagulls hovered above the deck ready to zoom down and snatch these treats from the passengers' hands. I was impressed with how the birds rode the air currents, coasting effortlessly up, down, and around. Surprised at how quickly this 45-minute trip passed, I pledged to bring some bread of my own for the return trip.

DW 29–DW 33

Answers will vary. Students should include as many sensory details as possible, attempt to write two introductions, and organize their paragraphs according to position, time order, or cause and effect.

IV

REPORT WRITING SKILLS AND ACTIVITIES

One of the more difficult tasks in school is report writing. Beginning with fourth grade, children are asked periodically to write reports on books or information related to content area subjects. In most cases students simply copy or paraphrase what they "read." Unfortunately, this practice is commonly accepted by teachers, and the problem continues through secondary school. The *Basic Composition Activities Kit* recognizes this and attempts to offer instructional alternatives.

The Report Writing section is designed to present a sequence of skills and activities that will enable students to organize the information and write it in a coherent, factual report. The progression of skills includes categorizing information, subordinating details and subtopics from topics, expanding notes or phrases into sentences, paragraphing by cause/effect, sequence, and comparison/contrast, and writing introductions and conclusions. Difficulty in any of these areas could result in problems with report writing. Therefore, teachers may choose to intervene, instruct, and assign practice in the skill areas if students require such assistance.

It is important to note that students are *not* required to locate either the sources or the information in this section. Notes are supplied in a random, disorganized list. Their job is to organize the notes and write an accompanying introduction and conclusion. When students have successfully mastered this system, they will be more inclined to adapt those techniques independently.

IV. REPORT WRITING SKILLS AND ACTIVITIES

CATEGORIZING I

Directions: There are 22 words listed below. These words can be grouped together into four categories with one word in each group as the "topic word." Write the topic word on the line at the top of each group. The other words in the group are "subtopic words" and are examples of the topic. Write those words underneath the appropriate topic word.

   Note: Some words might be used properly in more than one category. Be prepared to support your answers.

snake	butterfly	insect	wasp	giraffe
crab	animal	mosquito	fish	spider
goose	antelope	shrimp	bird	chicken
crow	cardinal	sparrow	trout	clam
	monkey		perch	

Topic Word: _____

_____

_____

_____

_____

_____

Topic Word: _____

_____

_____

_____

_____

_____

Topic Word: _____

_____

_____

_____

_____

Topic Word: _____

_____

_____

_____

_____

1. If you were to write a short one-paragraph report on each of these topics, how many paragraphs would you have? _____

2. What would be the topics of these paragraphs? _____

_____

3. Write a topic sentence for one of the paragraphs. _____

_____

4. Choose one of the categories and write a paragraph about it.

CATEGORIZING II

Directions: There are 18 words or phrases listed below. These words or phrases can be listed or grouped together in three categories. One word or phrase in each group will be the "topic word." Write the topic word on the line next to the roman numeral. The other words listed are "subtopic words" and are examples of the topic. Write these words underneath the appropriate topic. Use a dictionary if necessary.

handsome	happiness	feelings	applaud
comfortable	clumsy	muscular	tall
excitement	athletic	behavior	sorrow
compliment	ignore	joy	obese
physical characteristics	argue		

I. ————————————————   III. ————————————————

————————————————   ————————————————

————————————————   ————————————————

————————————————   ————————————————

————————————————   ————————————————

————————————————   ————————————————

II. ————————————————

————————————————

————————————————

————————————————

————————————————

————————————————

1. If you were to write a short one-paragraph report on each of these groups of words, how many paragraphs would you have? ————————————————

2. What would be the topics of these paragraphs? ————————————————

————————————————

3. Write a topic sentence for each of the paragraphs.

I. ————————————————

II. ————————————————

III. ————————————————

4. Now write *one* paragraph using one of your topic sentences and its subtopic words.

RW 2

TOPIC SENTENCES AND DETAILS I

Directions: Below you will read some details about an event. However, the notes do *not* include a main topic. *After reading* the notes, identify the topic of the information. *Then* write a good topic sentence. *Finally,* use this topic sentence as the beginning of a paragraph. Be sure to include all the notes in the paragraph and feel free to add your own ideas. Be sure to write in complete sentences.

Notes

chickens scurried to their pen
leaves rustled around the yard
my mother hurried to put garden tools away
huge, low-flying black clouds in western sky
bolt of lightning cracked in distance
gusts of wind blew open barn door
Father ran inside to close windows

Topic: _____

Topic Sentence: _____

_____

_____

_____

_____

_____

_____

_____

_____

_____

_____

_____

_____

_____

_____

_____

TOPIC SENTENCES AND DETAILS II

Directions: Read the four topic sentences listed below:

1. The last trip we took to _____ was _____.
2. My weekday schedule is monotonous and boring.
3. There are several reasons why _____ is my favorite season of the year.
4. On my way to school there are so many _____ sights to see.

Directions: Choose two of the topic sentences and expand each topic with seven specific details. List the details in the chart below.

Topic I: _____   Topic II: _____

D	D
E	E
T	T
A	A
I	I
L	L
S	S

Assignment: Write a four-to-six sentence paragraph using one of the topics above. Be sure to start with the topic sentence. Also make sure that your details follow in complete sentences.

_____

_____

_____

_____

_____

_____

_____

_____

DETAILS UNRELATED TO TOPIC

Directions: Read the following paragraphs carefully. Look for any problems in the paragraphs.

There are several advantages to owning a small car these days, yet there are still many good reasons why some people prefer to drive a larger car.

The benefits of a small car in today's world should be obvious. Most important, the ever-increasing cost of fuel encourages us to use less gas. Let's not be controlled by foreign oil producers. Smaller, lighter cars are much more fuel efficient than large cars, and some will even give you 50 miles on a gallon of gasoline. Since the car is smaller, it should cost us less to buy, operate, and maintain. If we want to reduce our dependence on foreign oil, then cutting gasoline usage is an effective way to do this.

However, an argument can be made in favor of big cars, too. A family larger than three or four would feel cramped in a small car, especially on a long trip. In addition, some people are convinced that large cars are safer and offer more protection than small ones. My whole family owns small cars. Furthermore, they say, you can enjoy a more comfortable ride in a heavier, larger vehicle. Those people who travel extensively like a comfortable car. The government cannot make us buy small cars.

In conclusion, each car buyer must make a decision as to which kind of car to buy after considering all of the advantages of each and his or her own needs. Which one would you choose?

What problems do you see in these paragraphs? Check the spaces below if you think there is a problem.

_____ 1. No introduction   _____ 3. Topic not clear

_____ 2. No conclusion   _____ 4. Details unrelated to topic

If you checked number four you are correct. There are sentences in paragraphs two and three that are NOT related to the topic sentences. Underline those sentences you feel are not related in each paragraph.

Are there any other problems in these paragraphs? Be specific. Share your responses.

_____

_____

_____

_____

_____

_____

_____

_____

_____

NOTES TO OUTLINE I

Directions: Listed below are several notes about birds. Three of these notes are listed as subtopics in the "Outline on Birds" which follows the notes. Write the details from the notes for each subtopic on the lines under A, B, and C.

Notes on Birds

Some birds travel thousands of miles to exact locations.

The physical characteristics of birds are very noticeable.

Their singing ability sets them apart from other animals.

Others have a low, raucous sound.

Mankind has been amazed at their ability to fly.

A number of birds imitate others when they sing.

These habits vary among birds, but they all follow regular routes.

Certain migratory habits are peculiar to birds.

Some birds' songs are high and shrill sounding.

Their feathery covering comes in many sizes and colors.

Outline on Birds

A. The physical characteristics of birds are very noticeable.

    1. _____

    2. _____

B. Their singing ability sets them apart from other animals.

    1. _____

    2. _____

    3. _____

C. Certain migratory habits are peculiar to birds.

    1. _____

    2. _____

Assignment: Write these notes in sentences and paragraphs. How many paragraphs will you have? Add relevant information if you want to expand the paragraph(s).

NOTES TO OUTLINE II

Directions: Listed below are notes about colonial fireplaces. Three of the notes are subtopics which you should write on lines A, B, and C in the outline following the notes. The other notes are details about each of the subtopics. Write these on the numbered lines below A, B, and C.

Notes for "How Colonial Fireplaces Were Used"

Hardwoods such as oak and maple gave the best heat.

Loaves of bread were baked in metal ovens built into the fireplace.

Children played games nearby.

Heating the house was an important use of the fireplace.

The fireplace was the center of family life during the winter.

Meat was roasted on a spit.

A huge supply of wood was burned during cold weather.

The family read the Bible and other books before the fire.

The fireplace was used for all the cooking of the food.

Vegetables were stewed in boiling pots hanging over the fire.

Ears of corn and potatoes were roasted in the hot ashes.

Visitors were entertained before the fire.

Outline for "How Colonial Fireplaces Were Used"

A. _____
  1. _____
  2. _____
  3. _____
  4. _____

B. _____
  1. _____
  2. _____
  3. _____

C. _____
  1. _____
  2. _____

Assignment: Write these notes in sentences and paragraphs. How many paragraphs will you have? Add relevant information if you want to expand the paragraph(s).

LOCATING SUBTOPICS AND DETAILS I

Directions: Read the following topic sentence:

"We can observe a number of different geometrical shapes in our daily lives."

Now read the notes listed below. There are three subtopics among the notes. Also, there are several details or examples of each subtopic. On the lines to the left of the notes, label the subtopics A, B, and C. Finally, write A-1, A-2, A-3, B-1, etc. next to the details that tell about each topic.

Notes

_____ steering wheels and tires

_____ spend many hours a week in front of television

_____ many examples of rectangular shapes to observe

_____ sails on sailboats, many tents are this shape

_____ even houses themselves have this shape

_____ circular shapes seen everywhere

_____ some men wear neckties with this kind of shape

_____ doors, windows examples of four-sided shape

_____ doughnuts eaten at breakfast

_____ shapes that resemble triangles are hard to find

_____ play games with balls of different sizes

_____ if live in city see many radio and TV towers

Assignment: Using the topic sentence above, write a paragraph or paragraphs including the subtopics and details you have numbered and lettered.

LOCATING SUBTOPICS AND DETAILS II

Directions: Read the following topic sentence:

"Mark Twain was one of America's most creative and prolific writers."

Now read the notes listed below. There are three subtopics among the notes. Also, there are several details or examples of each subtopic. On the lines to the left of the notes, label the subtopics A, B, and C. Finally, write A-1, A-2, A-3, B-1, etc. next to the details that tell about each subtopic.

Notes

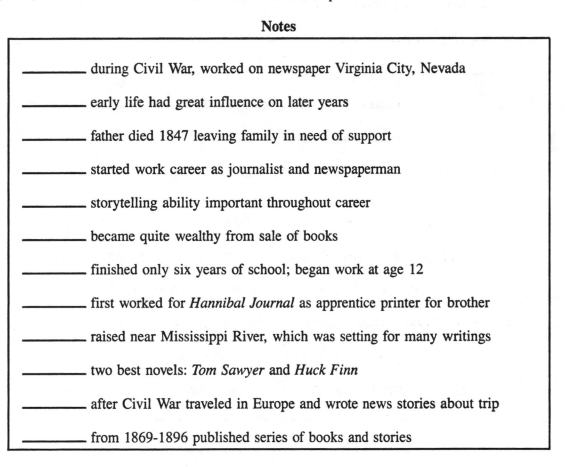

_____ during Civil War, worked on newspaper Virginia City, Nevada

_____ early life had great influence on later years

_____ father died 1847 leaving family in need of support

_____ started work career as journalist and newspaperman

_____ storytelling ability important throughout career

_____ became quite wealthy from sale of books

_____ finished only six years of school; began work at age 12

_____ first worked for *Hannibal Journal* as apprentice printer for brother

_____ raised near Mississippi River, which was setting for many writings

_____ two best novels: *Tom Sawyer* and *Huck Finn*

_____ after Civil War traveled in Europe and wrote news stories about trip

_____ from 1869-1896 published series of books and stories

Assignment: Using the topic sentence above, write a paragraph or paragraphs including the subtopics and details you have numbered and lettered.

LOCATING SUBTOPICS AND DETAILS III

Directions: Read the notes that are randomly listed in the box below. They include three subtopics along with several details or examples that relate to each subtopic. The main topic is *not* given. On the lines to the left of the notes, label the three subtopics A, B, and C. Then write A-1, A-2, A-3, B-1, etc. next to the details that tell about each subtopic.

Notes

_____ Doesn't require viewers to think

_____ Children may be misled by tricky or false advertising

_____ Television can be very entertaining and relaxing

_____ News reports keep us in touch with what's happening all around the world

_____ We can also learn much from television

_____ Programs like "National Geographic" are very informative as well as enjoyable

_____ Fun to watch people compete on game shows

_____ Programs that glorify violence and crime can influence a person's behavior

_____ Both kids and adults enjoy sports programs of all kinds

_____ On the other hand, television can have many harmful effects

_____ Keeps students from schoolwork and reading for pleasure

_____ Many children learn about history and literature by watching programs like "Little House on the Prairie"

Write a topic sentence for these notes: _____

_____

Assignment: Using these notes, write a report for your social studies class. Organize the A's, B's, and C's into separate paragraphs. Don't forget to write an introduction and a conclusion.

AUDIENCE I

Directions: Below are listed the facts about an accident that occurred recently in Springdale. You observed the accident as you were getting ready to cross an intersection.

Saturday, March 19, 1983, 6:30 p.m.
Sports car filled with young people driving behind station wagon
Elderly man and woman in station wagon driving south on Smith Street
Station wagon slowed down as if to stop
Sports car pulled out, accelerated to pass on left
No other cars on road
Station wagon turned left
Sports car tried to avoid wagon and crashed into tree
Station wagon made turn and came to stop

The information above is a series of facts. No judgments have been made about them. Read the two paragraphs about the incident and answer the questions that follow.

Paragraph A

As I was about to cross the intersection of Smith Street and Main Street in the Village of Springdale last Saturday, March 19, 1983, at 6:30 p.m., I observed the following. I first noticed a dark station wagon slowing down as it approached the intersection. It appeared that the car, driven by an elderly man, was going to stop. Then I saw a sports car pull outside to the left and accelerate, as if to pass. I could see there were several people in it. Next, the station wagon turned left and into the path of the faster-moving sports car. The driver of the sports car swerved away to avoid the other car and drove directly into a large tree. The wagon completed its turn and came to a stop without being hit.

Paragraph B

You wouldn't believe what I saw last Saturday night as I left Jennifer's house! This beat-up station wagon was creeping along Main Street to the corner of Smith Street. You really couldn't tell what the old goat who was driving was going to do. Next thing I heard and saw was Paul Jay's neat-looking Trans-Am pull around the wagon to pass. Well, that idiot in the wagon started to turn left and cut right in front of Paul's car. Paul swerved to avoid him and rammed right into that old maple tree on the corner. There were quite a few kids in Paul's car, but I guess no one was hurt seriously. You just can't trust these old people driving cars!

Questions:

1. Who was the audience in Paragraph A? _____

   Paragraph B? _____

2. Who was at fault according to Paragraph A? _____

   Paragraph B? _____

3. What kinds of judgments and opinions were made in Paragraph B that were not made in Paragraph A?

   _____

   _____

AUDIENCE II

Directions: Below are listed the facts about an accident that occurred recently in Springdale. The facts are the same as those listed in "Audience I."

Saturday, March 19, 1983, 6:30 p.m.
Sports car filled with young people driving behind station wagon
Elderly man and woman in station wagon driving south on Smith St.
Station wagon slowed down as if to stop
Sports car pulled out, accelerated to pass on left
No other cars on road
Station wagon turned left
Sports car tried to avoid wagon and crashed into tree
Station wagon made turn and came to stop

The information above is a series of facts. No judgments or opinions have been made about the people or objects involved. No judgment has been made about who is at fault.

Pretend that you are a 60-year-old man who has just left his bridge club and observes the accident on his way home. Write a description of the accident to a close friend. Write this description in a way that blames the young people for the accident.

_____

_____

_____

_____

_____

_____

_____

_____

_____

_____

_____

_____

WRITING INTRODUCTIONS I

Directions: Read the following situation for writing a report and compare it to the sample introduction. Then answer the questions that follow.

Situation: The principal, guidance counselor, and members of the English department are considering changing the present English curriculum. They have asked you to interview members of the student body to find out their opinion about changing from one 40-week subject to two 20-week subjects. You will then report your findings to the board of education.

Sample Introduction:

"As a member of the student council, I was asked by the principal, guidance counselor, and English department to interview students about a change in the English department curriculum. This change would allow students to choose two 20-week courses, rather than being assigned one 40-week course in English. The information below will highlight how the students feel about this proposed change."

How is the introduction similar to the situation? _____

How does the introduction differ from the situation? _____

Directions: Read the following situation for writing a report. Then write your own introduction.

Situation: You are the student council representative to the board of education. The board has discussed at its monthly meeting the possibility of *not* allowing students to drive their cars to school. You took notes on the discussion and now must report back to the student council the ideas discussed by the board.

Introduction:

_____

_____

_____

_____

_____

_____

_____

_____

_____

_____

_____

_____

WRITING INTRODUCTIONS II

Directions: The notes listed in the box below relate to the second situation described in Writing Introductions I. These notes will give you more information to include in an introduction. Read and organize the notes, then complete the assignment that follows.

Notes

Middle Valley High School cafeteria

April 8, 1983

students have constitutional right to drive

most student driving is unnecessary

might have to buy additional buses to carry extra students

quite a bit of disagreement on this topic

some students need quick transportation to after-school jobs

participants in extracurricular activities have unusual hours

superintendent asked a committee to look into pros and cons of this action

some use cars as escape to drink and/or take drugs

"All this extra driving is a waste of energy," according to Phil Hulton, taxpayer and parent

Assignment: Rewrite your introduction, if necessary, and then write the notes above as a report to the student council. Remember that as a reporter you are not supposed to include any of your own opinions in a report. You should include only facts from the meeting.

WRITING CONCLUSIONS I

Directions: Read the situation, sample introduction, and sample conclusion in Part A below. Notice how they are similar and how they are different. Discuss Part A with a partner, your teacher, or the class. Then read the situation and introduction for Part B and write a conclusion.

PART A:

Situation: You are a reporter for the school newspaper, the *Eagle Eye*, and you attended the November 17th AFS meeting. The foreign exchange student, Heidi Gensler, compared and contrasted life in Germany and in the United States. You wrote a news article for the *Eagle Eye* about this event.

Introduction: As your traveling reporter for the *Eagle Eye*, I attended the recent AFS meeting to hear our German exchange student, Miss Heidi Gensler. She presented a very humorous and informative lecture comparing American and German lifestyles.

Conclusion: In short, last Thursday's AFS meeting was one of the best in memory. Heidi's ability to make us laugh and listen at the same time made the hour-long presentation seem like five minutes. For those of you who could not attend, I hope you take the time to get to know Heidi.

PART B:

Situation: Your Modern Cultures class has been studying many different cultures throughout the world. The teacher has asked you to attend "Italian Night" and report your experiences to the rest of the class. All profits from this event, sponsored by the Hillside Rotary Club, will be donated to the Muscular Dystrophy Foundation. Many Rotarians will bring an Italian dish to share with others. Mr. Angelo Sabatini will also conduct a slide presentation on Italy.

Introduction: The Hillside Rotary Club sponsored "Italian Night" at the Hillside Regional High School last Wednesday night for the benefit of the Muscular Dystrophy Foundation. After the excellent dinner, Mr. Angelo Sabatini conducted a very educational slide presentation on the "People and Culture of Italy."

Conclusion:

_____

_____

_____

_____

WRITING CONCLUSIONS II

Information: Writing a conclusion is like writing someone a reminder. That is, you are reminding that person of what you have said before in just a few short words. Choosing those few short words is the key to writing a good conclusion. To find the words, do this: (1) identify the subtopics of your notes, (2) circle the key words in those subtopics, and (3) use those key words in your conclusion.

Directions: Read the notes on radar listed below. Identify subtopics A, B, and C. Circle the key words and use them in your conclusion. You may also want to use the "Conclusion Signal Words" shown in the box below to help you get started with the conclusion.

Notes on Radar

> _____ helps control airplane traffic at major airports
> _____ first developed 1935-40 as system for detecting position of remote objects by radio waves
> _____ used to navigate warships and bombers in all kinds of weather
> _____ peacetime uses of radar similar to military uses
> _____ improved immensely after World War II
> _____ can detect enemy aircraft at several hundred miles
> _____ military uses play important role in country's defense
> _____ used as aid in navigating large cargo ships in harbors
> _____ uses as a navigation and detection tool continuing to expand
> _____ also used for short-term weather forecasting
> _____ used in early warning system to protect North America from air invasion
> _____ newest use is in study of planets

Conclusion Signal Words

in conclusion	finally	consequently
in summary	in short	therefore
as you can see	to sum up	the information given above

Now write your conclusion:

_____

_____

_____

_____

FROM NOTES TO SENTENCES I

Information: Usually notes for a report are *not* taken in sentence and paragraph form. We jot them down quickly and in no specific order. When we want to use the notes we must first organize them by subtopic and detail. Then we need to rewrite them in complete sentences. When we do the rewriting, we ask ourselves three questions:

1. Are there any missing words, capital letters, or punctuation?

2. Can I combine any of the notes into one sentence?

3. Can I add any supplementary information or words?

Directions: Read and organize the following notes on your class trip to the Museum of Natural History. Asking yourself the three questions above, rewrite the notes in complete sentences.

Notes on Class Trip

Thursday morning, October 14, 1982
stopped at fast-food restaurant for lunch
wondered how people could have lived with so little
    machinery
took school bus to museum of Natural History in Rochester
wandered about museum for nearly two hours
different artifacts and remnants of early civilizations
Mr. Wetzel's social studies class went on field trip
amazed at old tools—could we use today?
class has studied several ancient civilizations
discussed trip when we returned to class
saw model of Egyptian shadoof, used to irrigate fields

FROM NOTES TO SENTENCES II

Information: Usually notes taken for a report are *not* written in sentence form. We jot them down quickly and in no specific order. First, you should organize the notes according to a plan. Then you should rewrite them in complete sentences.

Directions: Read the notes listed below. Number the notes in the order in which *you* think they happened. Then rewrite the notes in complete sentences. Remember to ask yourself three questions:

1. Are there any missing words, capital letters, or punctuation?

2. Can I combine any of the notes into one sentence?

3. Can I add any supplementary information or words?

Notes on Elizabeth Blackwell

_____ Elizabeth Blackwell, born 1819, died 1910
_____ real pioneer in struggle for women's rights
_____ started medical college to train women
_____ first woman doctor in U.S.
_____ very determined—would not give up
_____ accepted Geneva College of Medicine, Geneva, NY
_____ study continued—Paris, France; London, England
_____ very successful—worked hard for what she wanted
_____ practiced medicine in New York City first
_____ received first medical degree 1849—high honors
_____ wanted to study medicine—no school would let her
_____ established hospital—treated women and children

_____

_____

_____

_____

_____

_____

_____

_____

_____

ORGANIZING BY SEQUENCE I

Information: Writers present their material in several different ways. If their information is presented in a time order, we say that it follows a <u>sequence.</u> Many kinds of written material follow this pattern including news articles, police reports, and history books.

Directions: First, read the paragraph below and look for any words or phrases that signal time order or <u>sequence.</u> Then circle those words.

Mrs. James Wilson was guided to safety yesterday when a flight instructor radioed instructions for her to land the Piper Cub airplane in which she was a passenger. Mr. Wilson had collapsed from a heart attack while flying the single-engine plane home from their mountain vacation home. Immediately thereafter, Mrs. Wilson panicked. Then she yelled over the radio for someone to help her. At that time, a flight instructor just happened to hear her screams. First, he tried to calm her down by explaining the controls. Next, he helped her locate the position of the plane. He finally guided her in the right direction and convinced her that she could land the plane without any major problems. After a bumpy landing and a terrifying experience, Mrs. Wilson told reporters, "I guess somebody was with us up there!"

Directions: There are several words listed in the box below that act as time signals. Write your own account of an event that has taken place in or about your school or home. Use some of these time signals in your account. If you cannot think of a topic, look at your local newspaper for ideas.

first	then	after	immediately
next	when	before	simultaneously
finally	while	until	subsequently
last	as soon as	thereafter	at that time
	during		

_____

_____

_____

_____

_____

_____

_____

_____

_____

_____

_____

ORGANIZING BY SEQUENCE II

Directions: Read the situation and notes below, then write a report based on them. Present that report in the sequence or time-order organizational pattern. Use the sequence signal words. They help!

Situation: You attended the rock concert at the Carver High Auditorium. As a reporter for the school newspaper, you have to write an article about the concert for next week's edition.

Notes

_____ 12 people injured at rock concert
_____ played many hit tunes flawlessly for 2½ hours
_____ "Seats for future concerts will all be reserved," according to promoter John Horgan
_____ "Wayward Wrecking Company" performed December 3 at Carver High Auditorium
_____ crowd pushed and shoved to get tickets and best seats
_____ concert went on, as scheduled, but late start
_____ injured people rushed to River Road Hospital
_____ band not aware of what happened until after concert
_____ only a few seats reserved out of 1500 in auditorium

Assignment: Organize these notes according to sequence. Combine any notes that could go together in one sentence. Use any sequence signal words you need to make the article clear and accurate.

_____

_____

_____

_____

_____

_____

_____

_____

_____

_____

_____

ORGANIZING BY SEQUENCE III

Directions: Read the situation and notes below, then write a report based on them. Present that report in the sequence, or time-order pattern of organization. Use the sequence signal words ... they help!

Situation: You are one of four students in a geography class who took cross-country trips with their families last summer, beginning in New York State. Each of you will write a report to present to the class, so the entire class can compare your experiences.

Notes

- _____ visited Astrodome in Houston—watched Astros beat Mets
- _____ while in California, went to Disneyland and Hollywood
- _____ drove west to Grand Canyon National Park, Arizona—camped for two days
- _____ younger brother broke his leg at campsite near Cincinnati—got special treatment the rest of way home
- _____ our trip across country last summer was long but memorable
- _____ went southwest through Tennessee, Arkansas to Texas
- _____ family decided to visit Mount St. Helens in Washington even though we hadn't planned to go farther north
- _____ on to Las Vegas—won $50 in slot machine near campsite
- _____ drove across Midwest—couldn't believe the land in Iowa, Illinois, Indiana so flat—went miles without seeing a hill
- _____ began trip back east through Idaho to Yellowstone Park—camped two days at Old Faithful
- _____ drove up Pacific Coast to San Francisco—took great pictures of Bay Area Bridge
- _____ took trail down Grand Canyon to Colorado River—explored Indian pueblos
- _____ drove south through beautiful Blue Ridge Mountains of Virginia—camped there three days
- _____ trip from Las Vegas to Los Angeles through Mojave Desert helped me appreciate water and plant life

Assignment: Write this report according to the sequence of events. Use any sequence signal words you need to make your report clear and accurate.

ORGANIZING BY COMPARING AND CONTRASTING I

Information: Writers present their material in several different ways. If their writing shows how things or ideas are <u>alike</u> or <u>different,</u> they <u>compare</u> or <u>contrast</u> these things or ideas. Many types of written material, including social studies and science books, follow this pattern.

Directions: First read the paragraph below and look for any words or phrases that seem to <u>compare</u> or <u>contrast</u> the important ideas. Circle those words or phrases. Finally, answer the questions that follow.

The high schools of America are alike in many ways, yet there are some obvious differences among them. Most high schools are similar in that they require students to take basic subjects such as English, mathematics, social studies, and physical education. On the other hand, elective, or nonrequired, subjects vary greatly from school to school. City high schools often include only grades 10-12. In contrast, high schools in many rural towns or villages cover grades 7-12. Although there are a number of other differences among the schools, they all share the same basic goal—to prepare their students for the future.

1. What is being compared and contrasted?_____

2. In the paragraph above, what words or phrases signal when an idea will be compared or contrasted? List them below:

   _____

   _____

- -

Directions: Choosing one of the topics below, or any other topic you may prefer, write a paragraph *comparing* and/or *contrasting* two things or ideas. You may use any of the signal words found in the box at the bottom of the page.

   1. softball and baseball

   2. two members of your family

   3. eating at home and at a restaurant

   4. _____   ?

	Signal Words That Help Compare and Contrast	
similarly	in the same way	likewise
compared to	on the other hand	in contrast
in like manner	contrasted with	on the contrary

ORGANIZING BY COMPARING AND CONSTRASTING II

Directions: Read the situation and notes below, then, using the <u>compare/contrast</u> organizational pattern, write a report based on this information. Use the compare/contrast signal words ... they help!

Situation: You have recorded the notes below from many resources you found in the library and elsewhere. Use them to write a *one-paragraph* report on coal and oil for your geology teacher.

Notes

large supply of coal in U.S. greater than oil

oil needs to be pumped out of ground

two fossil fuels—coal and oil—have greater reserves
than all other countries

oil must be processed before used

coal used basically for generating energy

large percentage of oil comes from foreign countries

coal dug out of deep mines or stripped from surface

coal doesn't need any special treatment before use

oil used in production of many products, such as
plastics and lubricants

Assignment: Organize these notes by subtopic so you can compare and contrast the important ideas. Which notes go together? Then write a good topic sentence. Finally, use the compare/contrast signal words to help you organize the information in your one paragraph.

———————————————————————————————————————

———————————————————————————————————————

———————————————————————————————————————

———————————————————————————————————————

———————————————————————————————————————

———————————————————————————————————————

———————————————————————————————————————

———————————————————————————————————————

———————————————————————————————————————

———————————————————————————————————————

ORGANIZING BY COMPARING AND CONTRASTING III

Directions: Read the situation and notes below. Then, using the compare/contrast organizational pattern, write a report based on the information given. Use the compare/contrast signal words ... they help!

Situation: You have recorded the notes below during class and from information booklets on each of three sports. Your gym teacher wants you to write a report which will be presented to several foreign exchange students who will be attending your school.

Notes

11 players each side wearing heavy, protective equipment

played on diamond-shaped field which varies in size

football played in fall with professional championship games extending into January

basketball is fast-moving sport usually played in gym during winter months

played on field 100 yards long (excluding end zones) and 53 yards wide

three very popular sports enjoyed by Americans throughout the year

professional baseball season begins April—lasts until October with World Series

object to score touchdown worth six points, plus one point for the extra kick, and field goals worth three points

five players per team play both offense and defense

object to get as many batters as possible to hit ball safely and score runs

nine players space themselves around field to prevent opponents from hitting ball safely and scoring runs

all of these games played in schools, on playgrounds, and by professionals

object to score the most baskets in four quarters of play

Assignment: Organize these notes by subtopic so you can compare and contrast the important ideas. Use the compare/contrast signal words in your paragraphs.

ORGANIZING BY COMPARING AND CONTRASTING IV

Directions: Read the situation and notes below. Then, using the compare/contrast organizational pattern, write a report based on the information given. Use the compare/contrast signal words ... they help!

Situation: You have been asked by your health teacher to prepare a report on different kinds of drugs. This report will be presented to the fifth and sixth graders to inform them about the dangers of drug abuse.

Notes

stimulants are drugs that speed action of central nervous system

under drug influence we lose self-control—don't know what we're doing

barbiturates, known as "downers," slow reflexes, make sleepy

LSD, hashish, and PCP or "Angel Dust," can cause us to hallucinate, see things not there

long-term use of cocaine may cause depression, convulsions

all these drugs lead to mental dependency—hard to break

even mild depressants like alcohol, tobacco harmful to bodies

two examples of stimulants: cocaine and amphetamines

heroin and morphine are opiates—highly addictive, physically and mentally dangerous

hallucinogens change person's idea of what's happening

depressants such as barbiturates and opiates slow down central nervous system

"speed" is stimulant causing increased heart rate and pulse

Assignment: Organize these notes by subtopic so you can compare and contrast the important ideas. Use the compare/contrast signal words in your paragraphs.

ORGANIZING BY CAUSE AND EFFECT I

Information: Writers present their written material in several different ways. One of the patterns they use shows how certain events or ideas can *cause*, or lead to, another event. Many types of written material, including newspaper articles and science textbooks, follow this pattern.

Directions: First, read the paragraph below. Then look for any words or phrases that might signal when one event causes something else to happen. Circle those words or phrases. Finally, answer the questions that follow.

The early morning fire of April 10 at the Midlakes Junior High School has resulted in many problems for the district. Due to the intense heat generated from the fire, there was a great deal of structural damage to the auditorium. Consequently, most of the beams supporting the walls and the roof of this area must be replaced. Since smoke damage was very heavy in the seventh-grade wing of the building, all seventh-grade classes have had to be transferred to the Methodist Church Annex until further notice. Many citizens are upset because the newly installed fire alarm system failed to work properly, allowing the fire to burn out of control for nearly two hours before the fire department arrived. As a result of the fire, Superintendent of Schools, Dr. Philip Holgado, decided to close the school three days before the regularly scheduled spring vacation. This will allow the cleanup crew a few extra days to prepare for reopening on April 23.

1. List the words or phrases that you circled. _____

_____

2. How many of those words or phrases are included in the box of cause/effect signal words shown below?

_____

Directions: Choosing one of the topics listed below or any other topic you may prefer, write a cause/effect paragraph. You will find it helpful to use some of the signal words in the box at the bottom of this page.

1. a traffic accident
2. the blizzard of 1982
3. a power blackout
4. your choice

Cause and Effect Signal Words			
since	because of	thus	caused by
due to	consequently	so	as a result
because	therefore	if—then	for this reason

ORGANIZING BY CAUSE AND EFFECT II

Directions: Read the situation and notes below and write a report that uses the <u>cause/effect</u> organizational pattern. Use the cause/effect signal words. They help!

Situation: As a reporter for the *Valley View Herald,* you interviewed the mayor of Lower Malta after a recent storm. Your notes from the interview are in the box below.

Notes

overtime pay for city and county workers

bridge to hospital swept into river

local economy to suffer

winter wheat crop destroyed

Malta River overflowed

several farmers in lower valley lost livestock and machinery

will take many days to restore electric power

drinking water may be unsafe—must boil

early crops and fertilizers washed away

used up all emergency fund money in budget

Mayor Wilson requested all citizens to work together to recover from disaster

Assignment: First organize the notes by subtopic so you can group them in your paragraph(s). Then write a good topic sentence. Finally, use the cause/effect signal words in your paragraph(s) to help organize the information according to this pattern.

ORGANIZING BY CAUSE AND EFFECT III

Directions: Read the situation and notes below to write a report that uses the <u>cause/effect</u> organizational pattern. Use the cause/effect signal words . . . they help!

Situation: The students in a twelfth-grade health class have studied "Nutrition and Its Effect on Performance." They have also taken a survey of students and their eating habits. Some of the results of their study and survey are listed in the following notes. You have been asked to report these findings to the board of education.

Notes

> students eat poorly the rest of the day
>
> 39% of students surveyed had no breakfast at all
>
> students "high" on sugar can be behavior problems
>
> overweight people suffer from poor circulation, bad feet, and backaches
>
> even at home, snacks eaten were low in food value
>
> many come to school without a well-balanced breakfast
>
> 78% of those who eat school lunches do not eat the vegetables, fruits, or salads
>
> those without breakfast feel "lazy" and cannot concentrate
>
> snacks included foods high in sugar, salt and carbonation
>
> diabetes and high blood pressure can result from poor diet
>
> our feeling that board of education and parents should look further into this problem
>
> those who eat breakfast consume high quantities of sugar and carbohydrates
>
> can lead to school and health problems

Assignment: Organize these notes by subtopics so you can group the important ideas, using the cause/effect pattern. Then write a good introduction. Finally, use the cause/effect signal words to help you organize the information in paragraphs.

ORGANIZING BY CAUSE AND EFFECT IV

Directions: Read the situation and notes below and write a report using the <u>cause/effect</u> organizational pattern. Use the cause/effect signal words . . . they help!

Situation: As a member of the Work Study Program at school, you are required to write a report to the class about your experiences as a student nurse at the Wayne County Memorial Hospital. You wrote the following notes in preparing this report.

Notes

---

all volunteer—no pay

nurses don't panic, even under emergency conditions

must be good listener and encourage patients to talk about themselves

worked as student nurse afternoons since September

learned great deal about organization and operation of hospital

like to become registered nurse

met many friendly and dedicated people

nurses really run each floor and ward like clockwork

respect patience and knowledge of nursing staff

must not get too personally involved with patients and problems

hope to work in hospital full-time some day

Assignment: Organize these notes by subtopic so you can group the important ideas, using the cause/effect organizational pattern. Then write a good introduction. Finally, use the cause/effect signal words to help you organize the information in paragraphs.

REVISING I: MECHANICS

Information: When you write the first draft of a report, you are usually most interested in organizing the information in sentences and paragraphs. It is only natural to make mechanical errors in spelling, punctuation, capitalization, and grammar. Thus, it is important to read through the first draft carefully, looking for such errors. Many people read the first draft orally to see if it "sounds" right.

Directions: Read the paragraph below and look for any mechanical errors.

In our society, we do not live independantly of each other. A farmer in iowa may use a combine made in detroit michigan that Assembly line workers in detroit may wear clothes made from cotton grown by Alabama farmers and manufactured by workers in New York. The workers in New York will likely eat bread made from the wheat harvested by the Iowa farmer. we all depend on other people from different parts of the county for the things they need and want.

Check the kinds of errors that have been made in the paragraph:

_____ spelling   _____ capitalization   _____ words omitted

_____ punctuation   _____ grammar   _____ other

Assignment: Make any corrections necessary in the paragraph. Read it out loud to yourself to help you find any errors. Finally, rewrite the paragraph in final draft form.

_____

_____

_____

_____

_____

_____

_____

_____

REVISING II: EDITING

Information: When you write the first draft of a report, you are usually most interested in getting the information on paper. Sometimes you will put words or phrases in the wrong places, repeat ideas, forget to write an introduction or a conclusion, include unrelated information, or even write in a disorganized way. It is important to read your draft, looking for any of these problems.

Directions: Read the paragraph below and look for any editorial errors. Then check any problem areas that are included in the list following the paragraph.

Last Thursday I interviewed Dr. Jack Harris, after his entertaining and thoughtful assembly program on drug abuse in the Valleyview High School Auditorium. "This building does not look 15 years old. It's been well cared for," he remarked. Likewise, the whole school community appreciated his sense of humor and the message he left with us. His comments about our school were very complimentary. He was impressed with the condition and cleanliness of the school itself. Dr. Harris also made several positive statements about the students. "Their behavior and attention during the assembly was the best I have experienced in my eleven years of talking to students," he noted. Obviously, Dr. Harris enjoyed his short stay at Valleyview High School. The students' standing ovation at the conclusion of the assembly was especially satisfying to him.

_____ organization   _____ repetition of ideas

_____ words out of place   _____ introduction

_____ unrelated information   _____ conclusion

Assignment: Now rewrite the paragraph after editing any problems.

_____

_____

_____

_____

_____

_____

_____

_____

_____

_____

_____

_____

REVISING III: WORD CHOICE

Information: When you write the first draft of a report you are usually most interested in getting the information on paper. Therefore you don't always think of the best word or phrase to use.

Directions: Read the report below and underline any words or phrases that can be better expressed in fewer or more precise words. Also cross out any unnecessary words.

We had "Career Planning Day" at our school last week. It was sponsored by the Guidance Department, and many representatives from many areas spoke to us.

An Air Force recruiter said the Air Force was an excellent opportunity for advancement, for education, and for experience. However, the Navy recruiter said their program offered technical skill training and an opportunity to travel throughout the world. Several people from large corporations said they had training programs in sales, transportation and factory management. They all said there was a great opportunity with their companies. A local department store manager and supermarket manager also showed us how well we could do with them. They talked about opportunities within the several departments in their stores.

With all the choices and opportunities it will be hard to make a decision; but I did appreciate the opportunity to listen to what they all had to say.

Assignment: Rewrite this material in *one paragraph*, using a better selection of words. Eliminate those words or phrases you crossed out. Substitute more precise words for those you underlined.

_____

_____

_____

_____

_____

_____

_____

_____

_____

_____

_____

_____

REPORT WRITING: BIOGRAPHY I

Directions: The following notes on the life and times of Martin Luther King, Jr., were taken from three different sources. First, eliminate any information that is repeated, unimportant, or unrelated to the topic. Then organize the information according to subtopic and details.

SOURCE A

early life victim of racial prejudice

father Baptist minister

protested segregated buses, restaurants, other public places

became president of Southern Christian
Leadership Conference in 1958

noted for quote "I have a dream"

remembered today as champion of civil
rights

writings include "Why We Can't Wait"
(1964)

family not permitted to go anywhere or
do anything without discrimination

SOURCE B

mother was a school teacher

best noted for attacks on war,
poverty

born on January 15, 1929, in
Atlanta, Georgia

condemned Vietnam Conflict—too
many dollars spent, violence

his death had lasting effect on
U.S.

awarded Nobel Peace Prize (1964)

an eloquent and forceful speaker

was very popular in school

killed by assassin's bullet in
Memphis, Tennessee (1968)

SOURCE C

met wife Coretta in Boston (1953)

entered Morehouse College at age 15

believed nonviolent resistance

rioting by blacks in several U.S.
cities following assassination

birthday commemorated by millions of
Americans every year

at six years of age two white friends
not allowed to play with him
anymore

Assignment: Organize the notes from the three sources. Would you organize them according to sequence, compare/contrast, or cause/effect? Eliminate any information that is repeated, unimportant, or not related to the other subtopics. Then write this biographical report for your English teacher.

REPORT WRITING: BIOGRAPHY II

Directions: Below are three boxes in which you are to write notes from three different sources dealing with the life of John F. Kennedy. Above each box, write the source of the information, such as an encyclopedia, *Who's Who?*, an old magazine article, or a biography.

When you have finished taking notes, eliminate any information that is repeated, unnecessary, or unrelated to the topic. Then organize the notes by subtopic and details. Finally, write the report for your social studies class.

SOURCE A: _____

SOURCE B: _____

SOURCE C: _____

REPORT WRITING: BIOGRAPHY III

Directions: Below are three boxes in which you are to write notes from three different sources dealing with the life of Susan B. Anthony. Above each box, write the source of the information, such as an encyclopedia, *Who's Who?*, or a biography.

When you have finished taking notes, eliminate any information that is repeated, unnecessary, or unrelated to the topic. Then organize the notes by subtopic and details. Finally, write the report for your social studies class.

SOURCE A: _____   SOURCE B: _____

SOURCE C: _____

REPORT WRITING: PRACTICE AND REVIEW I

Directions: Write a report using the situation and notes given below.

Situation: You have taken the following notes from different sources for a report on "Species and Varieties of the Cat Family." This written report will be given to your science teacher.

Notes

several species and varieties of cats in world

includes wild species plus 30 breeds small domestic cats

spotted leopard commonly found in East Asia

known to be 2–2½' long, weigh up to 30 lbs.

more than 30 million domestic cats living in U.S. alone

lions found mainly in open plains of Africa

lion is a meat-eater known to kill zebras and antelopes

domestic cat one of earliest household pets

domestic is smallest of cat family—can still be wild and dangerous

farmers keep cats to control rat and mice populations in barns and houses

lion known as king of beasts

grayish-brown in color with many spots on body

adult lions grow to 300–500 pounds, 6–10' long

leopard hunts rodents and birds at night; sleeps days

Assignment: Organize these notes according to a plan. Which organizational pattern will you use?

Be sure to include all of the information in your report. Revise your notes before writing your final draft.

REPORT WRITING: PRACTICE AND REVIEW II

Directions: Write a report using the situation and notes given below.

Situation: You were present at a lecture by Dr. Richard Cole, entitled "Running—The Total Exercise." You took the following notes and intend to use them for writing an article for the school newspaper.

Notes

there are several physical benefits from running

many Americans unable to complete easy physical tests

feelings of depression disappear

produces a more cheerful outlook on life

helps body tolerate stress and strain

a real need for more exercise in America

will definitely increase energy level

most Americans devote little time to any activity

benefits skeletal muscles, the heart and lungs

the mental benefits are truly amazing

reduces one's desire for alcohol, tobacco, and food

many different kinds of exercise, running best

excellent for both men and women

Assignment: Organize these notes according to a plan. Which organizational pattern will you use?

_____

Be sure to include all of the information in your report. Revise your notes before writing your final draft.

REPORT WRITING: PRACTICE AND REVIEW III

Directions: Write a report using the situation and notes given below.

Situation: In social studies class you are studying the major religions of the world. You have been asked to research three of the most popular religions. The information you find will be reported to the class and will be compared with information on other religions that have been researched by others in the class. Your notes are listed below.

Notes

Hinduism has no single leader or person to follow

Buddhism is great oriental religion founded by Gautama Buddha

Muslims believe in just one God, Allah, and study bible called Koran

followers of Islam known as Mohammedans or Muslims

Hinduism one of world's great religions—more than 400 million followers

are several religions popular in world

believed to be 550-600 million Buddhists in world

they follow teachings of Mohammed much as Christians follow teachings of Christ

Buddhism started in India, but today most popular in China, Japan, and Southeast Asia

most Hindus live in India

Islam is religion of over 500 million Arabs from Africa, Asia, and Middle East

serve, respect, and idolize their God, Buddha

hundreds of gods, common to every Indian household

Assignment: Organize these notes according to a plan. Which organizational pattern will you use?

Be sure to include all of the information in your report. Revise your notes before writing your final draft.

REPORT WRITING: PRACTICE AND REVIEW IV

Directions: Write a report using the situation and notes given below.

Situation: As part of an English class assignment, you are to write a report on a favorite hobby or interest. Your notes about gardening are listed below.

Notes

plant seeds

be sure vegetables are ripe before harvesting

watch out for pests that kill and eat plants

before planting seeds, prepare soil and line up rows

planning the garden begins in February

read seed packets to see best time to plant; mark calendar

don't plant seeds too shallow or deep

if planned and cared for will yield fine crop of fresh produce

must measure and plot garden space

decide what to plant and order through catalog company

tamp down soil gently on top seeds and water

when plants are young, cultivate to keep weeds out

Assignment: Organize these notes according to a plan. Which organizational pattern will you use?

Be sure to include all of the information in your report. Revise your notes before writing your final draft.

REPORT WRITING: PRACTICE AND REVIEW V

Directions: Write a report using the situation and notes given below.

Situation: You have been asked to prepare a report for your science/health teacher on various oils and their uses. Below are the notes you took from several different sources.

Notes

> most animal oils or fats not consumed
>
> soybean oil single most important oil product in world
>
> corn oil used to make mayonnaise and salad dressings
>
> various kinds of oils found in nature
>
> marine or water-type oils not normally used for eating
>
> lard a major animal oil—comes from hogs
>
> oil from whale's blubber for cosmetics, some drugs
>
> tallows and greases are fats from hogs
>
> more than ten different kinds of vegetable oils
>
> most fish oils used in paint products, lubricating greases
>
> peanut oil second largest eaten worldwide
>
> after cream separated from cow's raw milk we get butterfat

Assignment: Organize these notes according to a plan. Which organizational pattern will you use?

_____

Be sure to include all of the information in your report. Revise your notes before writing your final draft.

REPORT WRITING: OUTLINE FORM

Topic _____ Audience _____

Type of organization _____

(sequence, compare/contrast, cause/effect)

Introduction _____

_____

_____

Suptopic #1 _____

_____

Details about #1 _____

_____

_____

_____

Subtopic #2 _____

_____

Details about #2 _____

_____

_____

_____

Subtopic #3 _____

_____

Details about #3 _____

_____

_____

_____

Conclusion _____

_____

_____

_____

_____

REPORT WRITING TOPICS

Classroom or School Activities

curricula	cafeteria
extracurricular activities	any department
rules and policies	favorite subject
athletics	worst subject
assemblies	issues or problems
homework	testing

Individual Interests

family	part-time job
hobbies	parents' occupations
sports	television or radio programs
pets	neighborhood
music and art	books or magazines

Past Experiences

visit to historical attraction or national monument
feelings about something
movie seen in or out of school
most embarrassing, humorous, frightening, or disappointing experience
an earlier teacher or friend

Content Area Subjects

Use specialized vocabulary in sentences or paragraphs.
Summarize a topic, chapter, or unit.
Explain a cause and effect relationship.
Write topic sentences and related paragraphs about randomly organized details.
Write to someone outside of school for more detailed information.
Support or reject statements made in subject area.

Literature

Describe setting.	Compare and contrast two characters.
Describe character appearance.	Summarize plot.
Describe character behavior.	

Current Events

energy	government action or inaction
conservation	government services
education	strikes
taxation	the draft
drug abuse	court cases
national/international conflicts	

REPORT WRITING: SIGNAL WORDS

Sequence

first	after
next	before
finally	until
last	thereafter
then	immediately
when	simultaneously
while	subsequently
as soon as	at that time
during	

Cause and Effect

since	thus
due to	so
because	if—then
because of	caused by
consequently	as a result
therefore	for this reason

Compare and Contrast

similarly	contrasted with
compared to	likewise
in like manner	in contrast
in the same way	on the contrary
on the other hand	

Conclusion

in conclusion	to sum up
in summary	consequently
as you can see	therefore
finally	the information given above
in short	

ANSWER KEY

RW 1

Topic word: Animal. Subtopic words: snake, crab, antelope, monkey, giraffe.
Topic word: Fish. Subtopic words: shrimp, trout, perch, clam.
Topic word: Insect. Subtopic words: butterfly, mosquito, wasp, spider.
Topic word: Bird. Subtopic words: goose, crow, cardinal, sparrow, chicken.
1. four.
2. animal, insect, fish, bird.
3. Animal life on earth is very diverse.
4. Answers will vary.

RW 2

  I. Topic word: physical characteristics. Subtopic words: athletic, handsome, muscular, tall, obese.
 II. Topic word: feelings. Subtopic words: comfortable, excitement, happiness, joy, sorrow
III. Topic word: behavior. Subtopic words: clumsy, ignore, argue, applaud.
1. three.
2. physical characteristics, feelings, behavior.
3. I. Each of us has distinct physical characteristics.
    II.Our feelings range from pleasurable to unpleasurable.
    III.Our behavior is influenced by many internal and external stimuli.
4. Answers will vary

RW 3

Topic: The Coming Storm.
Topic sentence: A thunderstorm suddenly appeared as we were working in the garden.
Huge, low-flying black clouds spread across the western sky, and a bolt of lightning cracked in the distance. Leaves rustled around the yard and gusts of wind blew open the barn door. The chickens scurried to their pen. My mother hurried to put the garden tools away, and father ran inside to close windows.

RW 4

Answers will vary. Sample:
1. New York City, exciting

3. spring.
4. special.

Topic I: New York City. Details: week of spring vacation
                                  visited World Trade Center
                                  boat trip around Manhattan
                                  climbed Statue of Liberty
                                  horse and buggy ride through Central Park
                                  saw two plays
                                  tour of United Nations

Topic III: Spring. Details: end of cold weather
                                  everything turns green and begins to grow again
                                  put away heavy clothing
                                  baseball team
                                  bicycling and fishing
                                  planning for vacation
                                  end of school nearing

    The last trip we took to New York City was exciting. My father, mother, sister, and I spent a whole week of spring vacation just exploring the city. We visited the twin towers of the World Trade Center, 110 stories high. We took a boat trip around Manhattan, climbed the Statue of Liberty, toured the United Nations, and rode through Central Park in a horse and buggy. We also saw two Broadway plays. Every day was packed with new experiences.

RW 5

Sentences underlined:
    Let's not be controlled by foreign oil producers.
    If we want to reduce our dependence on foreign oil, then cutting gasoline usage is an
        effective way to do this.
    My whole family owns small cars.
    The government cannot make us buy small cars.
Other problem: In each paragraph, the same information is repeated.

RW 6

A.
    1. Mankind has been amazed at their ability to fly.
    2. Their feathery covering comes in many sizes and colors.

B.
    1. Some birds' songs are high and shrill sounding.
    2. Others have a low, raucous sound.
    3. A number of birds imitate others when they sing.

C.

1. These habits vary among birds, but they all follow regular routes.

2. Some birds travel thousands of miles to exact locations.

Assignment: Answers will vary.

RW 7

A. The fireplace was used for all the cooking of the food.

1. Loaves of bread were baked in metal ovens built into the fireplace.

2. Meat was roasted on a spit.

3. Vegetables were stewed in boiling pots hanging over the fire.

Ears of corn and potatoes were roasted in the hot ashes.

B. The fireplace was the center of family life during the winter.

1. The family read the Bible and other books before the fire.

2. Children played games nearby.

3. Visitors were entertained before the fire.

C. Heating the house was an important use of the fireplace.

1. A huge supply of wood was burned during cold weather.

2. Hardwoods such as oak and maple gave the best heat.

Assignment: Answers will vary.

RW 8

A-1, B-3, B, C-1, B-2, A, B-4, B-1, A-2, C, A-3, C-2.

Answers will vary. Sample:

We can observe a number of different geometrical shapes in our daily lives. Circular shapes are seen everywhere—in steering wheels and tires, in doughnuts eaten at breakfast, in the balls of different sizes used in various games. There are also many examples of rectangular shapes to observe. They can be found in doors, windows, houses, television screens, even the neckties worn by some men. Examples of triangular shapes are less common. They include sails on sailboats, some tents, and radio and television towers.

RW 9

B-2, A, A-2, B, C, C-3, A-3, B-1, A-1, C-2, B-3, C-1.

Answers will vary. Sample:

Mark Twain was one of America's most creative and prolific writers. Mark Twain's early life had a great influence over his later years. He was raised near the Mississippi River, which was the setting for many of his writings. His father died in 1847, leaving his family in need of support. Mark Twain finished only six years of school and began work at the age of twelve.

Mark Twain started his work career as a journalist and newspaperman. He first worked for the *Hannibal Journal* as an apprentice printer for his brother. During the Civil War, he worked on a newspaper in Virginia City, Nevada. After the war, he traveled in Europe and wrote news stories about his trip.

Twain's storytelling ability was important throughout his career. From 1869–1896 he published a series of books and stories. His two best novels were *Tom Sawyer* and *Huck Finn*. He became quite wealthy from the sale of his books.

RW 10

C-1, C-2, A, B-2, B, B-3, A-1, C-3, A-2, C, C-4, B-1.
Answers will vary. Sample:

Television viewing can have both beneficial and harmful effects. Being aware of these effects should help all of us become wiser viewers.

Watching television can be very entertaining and relaxing. It is fun to watch people compete on game shows. Both kids and adults enjoy sports programs of all kinds.

We can also learn much from television. Many children learn about history and literature from watching programs like "Little House on the Prairie." News reports keep us in touch with what's happening all around the world. Programs like "National Geographic" are very informative as well as enjoyable.

On the other hand, television can have many harmful effects. It doesn't require viewers to think. Children may be misled by tricky or false advertising. Programs that glorify violence and crime can influence a person's behavior. Watching television also keeps students from schoolwork and reading for pleasure.

In short, television can be a very powerful means of entertainment and education, but can also have a number of damaging effects on young and old alike.

RW 11

1. Paragraph A: police officer. Paragraph B: Friend of sports car driver.
2. Paragraph A: no one at fault. Paragraph B: elderly couple at fault.
3. The driver of the sports car was not at fault. Old people are not reliable drivers.

RW 12

Answers will vary. Sample:

I saw a carful of young hotshots cause another accident on Saturday night, right after I left my bridge club. They were driving behind an elderly couple in a station wagon, in one of those jazzed-up sports cars. Then, just as the wagon began to slow down to turn left on Smith Street, these young fools barrelled out and started to pass. The wagon turned left and the kid driving the sports car swerved and drove head-on into the big maple tree on the corner. The couple in the wagon stopped to see if they could help, but luckily no one was seriously hurt. These crazy kids are a menace on the road.

RW 13

Same basic information
Written in first person
Sample introduction:

As the student council representative to the board of education, I was present at the recent board meeting at which the topic of student driving came up. The members of the board discussed the possibility of *not* allowing students to drive their cars to school. The following is a brief report of the ideas discussed at the meeting.

RW 14

As the student council representative to the board of education, I attended the board's meeting of April 8, 1983, in the Middle Valley High School cafeteria, at which the topic of student driving was considered. The members of the board discussed the possibility of not allowing students to drive their cars to school. The following is a brief report of the ideas that were presented at the meeting.

Several members of the board began the discussion by voicing their belief that most student driving is unnecessary. Mr. Phil Hulton, a taxpayer and parent, then said, "All this extra driving is a waste of energy." One of the members also stated that some students use cars as an escape to drink and/or take drugs.

Other board members then pointed out that students have a constitutional right to drive and that preventing them from driving their cars to school would be a hardship to some students and, possibly, to the school district. They pointed out that some students need quick transportation to after-school jobs and that students who participate in extracurricular activities have unusual hours. They also noted that the system might have to buy additional buses to carry extra students.

Since there was quite a bit of disagreement on the topic, the superintendent asked a committee to look into the pros and cons of banning student driving to school. The committee is to report at the next meeting of the board.

RW 15

Sample conclusion:

In summary, last Wednesday's "Italian Night" gave me new insights into the culture of Italy. I discovered a variety of Italian foods and learned many new things about the country and people of Italy.

RW 16

C, A, B, C, A, B, B, C, A, C, B, C
Key words circled: peacetime uses, military uses, navigation and detection.
Sample conclusion: as you can see, radar systems have many important military and peacetime uses in air and sea navigation and detection.

RW 17

Sample:

On Thursday morning, October 14, 1982, I went on a field trip by school bus to Rochester to the Museum of Natural History with Mr. Wetzel's social studies class. At the museum, we wandered about for nearly two hours looking at different artifacts and remnants of early civilization. For example, we saw a model of an Egyptian shadoof, used to irrigate fields. All of us were amazed at the old tools and wondered if we could use them today. We also wondered how people could have lived with so little machinery.

On the way back to school we stopped at a fast-food restaurant for lunch. When we returned to class we discussed the trip and what we have learned from our studies of several ancient civilizations.

RW 18

1, 3, 12, 2, 5, 6, 8, 10, 9, 7, 4, 11
Answers will vary. Sample:

Elizabeth Blackwell, 1819–1910, was the first woman doctor in the United States and a real pioneer in the struggle for women's rights. When she first wanted to study medicine, no school would let her. However, she was very determined and would not give up. Finally, she was accepted at Geneva College of Medicine in Geneva, New York, and received her first medical degree in 1849 with high honors. Dr. Blackwell continued her study in Paris, France, and London, England.

She first practiced medicine in New York City and, because she worked hard for what she wanted, was very successful. Later, she established a hospital for the treatment of women and children and started a medical college to train women.

RW 19

Words circled: yesterday, while, Immediately thereafter, Then, At that time, First, Next, finally, After.
Answers will vary. Sample:

When Phil asked me to the Junior Prom, I was a little hesitant because he was so shy. On prom night, first we went to the Captain's Cove for a delicious seafood dinner. At that time he didn't talk too much; the others in our party dominated the discussion.

As soon as we arrived at the dance and sat down, I found that Phil was an excellent conversationalist. I guess he really likes to listen to other people because he asked me so many questions. Before the end of the evening I learned much about Phil, too. If he asks me out in the future, I'm sure I'll answer "yes" immediately.

RW 20

1, 6, 9, 3, 2, 5, 4, 7, 8
Answers will vary. Sample:

Twelve people were injured in the push and shove to get tickets and the best seats for the "Wayward Wrecking Company" rock concert at Carver High Auditorium on December 3. The injured people were rushed to River Road Hospital and the concert went on as scheduled, but got a late start.

The band played many tunes flawlessly for 2½ hours, unaware of what had happened until after the concert. Only a few seats had been reserved in the auditorium, which holds 1500 people. According to promoter John Horgan, "Seats for future concerts will all be reserved."

RW 21

4, 9, 5, 14, 1, 3, 11, 7, 13, 12, 10, 6, 2, 8
Answers will vary. Sample:

Our trip across country last summer was long but memorable. First, we drove south through the beautiful Blue Ridge Mountains of Virginia and camped there three days. Then we went southwest through Tennessee and Arkansas to Texas. In Houston we visited the Astrodome and watched the Astros beat the Mets. Next we drove west to the Grand Canyon National Park in Arizona where we camped for two days. While there, we took a trail down the canyon to the Colorado River and explored some Indian pueblos. We went on to Las Vegas, where I won $50 in a slot machine near our campsite. The trip from Las Vegas to Los Angeles through the Mojave Desert helped me appreciate water and plant life.

While in California, we went to Disneyland and Hollywood. Then we drove up the Pacific Coast to San Francisco. I took some great pictures of the Bay Area Bridge. Our family then decided to visit Mount St. Helens in Washington even though we hadn't planned to go farther north.

We began the trip back east through Idaho to Yellowstone Park and camped two days at Old Faithful. Next, we drove across the Midwest. I couldn't believe the land in Iowa, Illinois, and Indiana was so flat. We went for miles without seeing a hill. My younger brother broke a leg at our campsite near Cincinnati and got special treatment the rest of the way home.

RW 22

Words circled: similar, On the other hand, In contrast, share.
1. American high schools.
2. similar, On the other hand, In contrast, share.
Answers will vary. Sample:

My brothers Frank and Jerry are identical twins. They look exactly like each other but are almost completely different in every other way. Frank is good in art but just gets by in his other subjects. He doesn't enjoy sports and spends most of his time after school with a few friends or building things at home. My father calls him a dreamer. In contrast, Jerry gets high marks in all of his courses and plays sports after school from September to June. He is always with a gang of friends and drives my parents wild because he never wants to stay at home. While Frank is the "dreamer" of the twins, Jerry, on the other hand, is the "mover." Identical twins couldn't be more different!

RW 23

Answers will vary. Sample:

Of the two fossil fuels—coal and oil—the U.S. has greater reserves than any other country in the world. The large supply of coal in our country is greater than the oil supply. The coal is dug out of deep mines or stripped from the surface. It is used basically for generating energy. It doesn't need any special treatment before it is used as fuel. Much of the oil consumed in our country comes from foreign countries. Oil must be pumped out of the ground. It is used in the production of many products, such as plastics and lubricants, as well as for energy. Oil must be processed before it is used.

RW 24

Answers will vary. Sample:

There are three very popular sports enjoyed by Americans throughout the year. Even though baseball, football, and basketball are very different, hundreds of thousands of Americans either watch or participate in these sports.

The professional baseball season begins in April and lasts until the October World Series. It is played on a diamond-shaped field, which varies in size. Nine players space themselves around this field to prevent their opponents from hitting the ball and scoring runs. The other team tries to get as many batters as possible to hit the ball safely and score runs.

In contrast, football is played in the fall with professional championships like the "Super Bowl" extending into January. The playing field is 100 yards long (excluding the end zones) and 53 yards wide. There are 11 players on each side, wearing heavy, protective equipment. The object of the game is to score touchdowns, worth six points, plus one point for the extra kick, and three points for a field goal.

Unlike baseball and football, basketball is a fast-moving sport usually played in a gymnasium during the winter months. There are only five players per team that play both offense and defense at the same time. The purpose of the game is to score the most baskets in four quarters of play.

In conclusion, all of these games are played widely in schools, on playgrounds, and by professionals. Whether Americans are spectators or participants, baseball, football, and basketball are three of America's most popular sports.

RW 25

Answers will vary. Sample:

Several types of drugs can be very harmful to our health and our bodily systems. Before you try any of these, you should be aware of what they are and how they affect us.

The first kind are stimulants. These are drugs that speed up the central nervous system. Two examples you have probably heard about are cocaine and amphetamines. (Long-term use of cocaine may cause depression and convulsions.) Another stimulant is "speed," which causes increased heart and pulse rates. Similar to the stimulants are hallucinogens, which can change a person's idea of what is happening. Drugs like LSD, hashish, and PCP or "angel dust" can cause a user to hallucinate, or see things that aren't really there.

On the other hand, depressants, such as barbiturates and opiates, slow down the nervous system. Barbiturates, also known as "downers," slow reflexes and make a person sleep. Even mild depressants like alcohol and tobacco are harmful. Heroin and morphine are the major opiates, and they are highly addictive as well as physically and mentally dangerous.

As you can see, depressants, stimulants, and hallucinogens can be dangerous drugs to use. Under their influence we lose self-control and harm our bodily systems. In addition, these drugs lead to mental dependency, which is hard to break.

RW 26

1. Words circled: has resulted in, Due to, Consequently, Since, because, As a result.
2. five
Answers will vary. Sample:

The blizzard of 1982 was a disaster in our city. It began one Thursday morning about 9 a.m. Because snow was piling up so fast, most schools sent their students home early. By evening rush hour, the roads were snow-covered and slippery. Consequently, there were scores of accidents on all the major highways. The 40- to 50-mile-per-hour winds caused near-zero visibility. Usually these winter storms slow down after 24 hours, but the blizzard of 1982 continued through the weekend. As a result, our city didn't return to normal for two weeks.

RW 27

Answers will vary. Sample:

Ralph Wilson, Mayor of Lower Malta, gave a gloomy report on the aftermath of last week's cloudburst. Since the Malta River overflowed, the bridge to the hospital was swept away. In addition, several power lines came down and it will take a few more days to restore electric power in some parts of the city. Because some of the water supply may have been contaminated, citizens have been urged to boil their drinking water.

Mayor Wilson also reported that our local economy may suffer. Farmers in the lower valley lost livestock and machinery, and much of the winter wheat crop was destroyed. Several farmers noted that their early plantings and fertilizers were also washed away. Mayor Wilson stated that the emergency fund money in the budget will likely be used up in order to pay overtime wages for all of the city and county road crews. In a final note, the Mayor has requested that all citizens work together to help the city recover from this disaster.

RW 28

Answers will vary. Sample:

After studying "Nutrition and Its Effect on Performance," our twelfth-grade health class conducted a survey of student eating habits. We would like to report the results of that survey together with a few conclusions.

Many students come to school without a well-balanced breakfast. Those who do eat breakfast consume high quantities of sugar and carbohydrates. However, 39 percent of the students surveyed had no breakfast at all. As a result, these people feel "lazy" and cannot concentrate as well.

According to the survey, most students eat poorly the rest of the day. Seventy-eight percent of those who eat school lunches skip the vegetables, fruits, or salads. Even at home, the snacks included valueless foods high in salt, sugar, and carbonation.

As a result of our studies in health class, we have learned that poor diet leads to school and health problems. For example, students "high" on sugar can be behavior problems. Overweight people suffer from poor circulation, backaches, and bad feet. Furthermore, diabetes and high blood pressure can result from poor diet.

It is our opinion, therefore, that the board of education and parents should look into this situation further. Nutrition does have an effect on performance and we should all try to impress this upon the students and families in our district.

RW 29

Answers will vary. Sample:

My work as a volunteer student nurse at The Wayne County Memorial Hospital was both enjoyable and informative. The work-study program helped me to understand much more about hospital operations. It also convinced me that a future in hospital work would be a satisfying career.

I learned a great deal about the organization and operation of a hospital as a result of this experience. Nurses run each floor and ward like clockwork, and they never panic—even in an emergency. As hospital employees, they must be good listeners and encourage patients to talk about themselves. However, it is important not to get too personally involved with patients and their problems. Because I spent so much time with the nurses, I learned to respect their patience and knowledge.

The work-study program helped me to decide how much I'd like to work in a hospital full-time, possibly as a registered nurse. As a volunteer, I wasn't rewarded with money for working every afternoon since September. But meeting all those friendly and dedicated people was well worth the effort.

RW 30

Errors: spelling, punctuation, capitalization, grammar, other.
Answers will vary. Sample:

In our society we do not live independently of each other. A farmer in Iowa may use a combine made in Detroit, Michigan. Assembly line workers in Detroit may wear clothes made from cotton grown by Alabama farmers and manufactured by workers in New York. The workers in New York will likely eat bread made from wheat harvested by the Iowa farmer. We all depend on people from different parts of the country for the things we need and want.

RW 31

Problem areas: organization, unrelated information, conclusion.
Answers will vary. Sample:

Last Thursday I interviewed Dr. Jack Harris after his entertaining and thoughtful assembly program on drug abuse in the Valleyview High School Auditorium. His comments about our school were very complimentary. He was impressed with the condition and cleanliness of the school itself. "This building does not look 15 years old. It's been well cared for," he remarked. Dr. Harris also made several positive statements about the students. "Their behavior and attention during the assembly was the best I have experienced in my eleven years talking to students," he noted. The students' standing ovation at the conclusion of the assembly was especially satisfying to him. Obviously, Dr. Harris enjoyed his short stay at Valleyview High School.

RW 32

Answers will vary. Sample:

We attended "Career Planning Day" at our school last week. It was sponsored by the Guidance Department, and several representatives spoke to us. An Air Force recruiter noted the Air Force provided an excellent opportunity for advancement, education, and experience. However, the Navy recruiter said their program offered technical skill training and world travel. Representatives from large corporations outlined training programs in sales, transportation, and factory management. In addition, a local department store manager and supermarket owner highlighted careers within the departments of their stores. With all these choices, it will be hard to make a decision, but I did appreciate listening to what they had to say.

RW 33

Answers will vary. Sample organized in sequence:

The son of a Baptist minister and a school teacher, Dr. Martin Luther King, Jr., was born on January 15, 1929, in Atlanta, Georgia. In his early life, Martin was a victim of racial prejudice. When he was six years old, two white friends were not permitted to play with him anymore. In addition, his family was not permitted to go anywhere or do anything without discrimination.

Martin believed in nonviolent resistance to this racial discrimination and he protested segregated buses, restaurants, and other public places. But he was best known for his attacks on war and poverty. King became president of the Southern Christian Leadership Conference in 1958 because he was such an eloquent and forceful speaker. He is best remembered for his "I have a dream" speech. He condemned the violence and dollar waste of the Vietnam Conflict and was awarded the Nobel Peace Prize in 1964.

Dr. King was killed by an assassin's bullet in Memphis, Tennessee in 1968 and his death has had a lasting effect on the United States. Rioting by angry blacks began in several U.S. cities following the assassination. Today he is remembered as a champion of civil rights and his birthday is commemorated by millions of Americans every year.

RW 34

Answers will vary. Sample:

Source A: Kane, *Facts About Presidents*
  born Brookline, Massachusetts May 1917
  educated Choate Academy, Harvard University
  served World War II as Navy lieutenant
  Congressman from Massachusetts 1946–1950
  Senator from 1952–1960
  elected President 1960, youngest ever elected
  first Roman Catholic president
  assassinated by Lee Harvey Oswald November 22, 1963

Source B: *Encyclopedia International*
  thirty-fifth president, beat Richard Nixon 1960
  author, wrote *Profiles in Courage* (1954) about former Congressmen who risked reelection
    for own beliefs
  celebrated hero in World War II when boat (PT 109) sunk by Japanese; saved several crew
    members
  gained public support for U.S. space program
  won Pulitzer Prize for *Profiles in Courage*

Source C: Manchester, *Portrait of a President*
  Inaugural Address dedicated to a "struggle against enemies of man: tyranny, poverty,
    disease, and war"
  thirty-fifth president 1961–1963
  initiated Peace Corps to aid underdeveloped countries
  started Alliance for Progress
  introduced Civil Rights Bill 1963, but not passed until after his death
  forced Russians out of Cuba with a quarantine in 1962
  highly respected as president, untimely death mourned by all

John Fitzgerald Kennedy, 35th President of the U.S., was born in Brookline, Massachusetts in 1917. Educated at Choate Academy and Harvard University, he was well-prepared for a life in public service.

Kennedy served in World War II as a lieutenant in the Navy. While on duty in a Navy patrol boat, PT 109, the Japanese sunk his ship. He rescued several members of the crew and was later decorated as a war hero. In 1946, Kennedy was elected to the House of Representatives, and won reelection two times. During his first term as a Senator, he wrote a Pulitzer Prize-winning book, *Profiles in Courage,* praising several courageous former Congressmen.

The youngest man ever elected as president, Kennedy beat Richard Nixon in 1960. In his Inaugural Address he dedicated his presidency to "a struggle against the common enemies of man: tyranny, poverty, disease, and war." One accomplishment was initiation of the Peace Corps to aid underdeveloped countries of the world. He also started the Alliance for Progress, which attempted to help Latin American countries improve their standard of living. In 1962, he made a bold move to force the Russians out of Cuba. The next year, Kennedy introduced the Civil Rights Bill of 1963, but never lived to see it made law. Unfortunately, Kennedy was assassinated by Lee Harvey Oswald on November 22, 1963, before he finished his term of office. Respected by millions of people, his death was mourned by all.

RW 35

Answers will vary. Sample:

Source A: *Dictionary of American Biography*
> born February 1820 in Adams, Massachusetts
> Quaker family encouraged independence and self-confidence
> eager student, learned to read and write early
> successful teacher and administrator at Canajoharie Academy
> first public efforts in the temperance movement
> early days not allowed to speak in public
> fought for passage of 14th Amendment, voting rights for blacks
> pushed for equal rights for women

Source B: Lutz, *Susan B. Anthony: Rebel, Crusader, Humanitarian*
> American feminist and reformer
> spent most of life in New York State but traveled widely
> never married, dedicated life to important social causes and reform
> influenced by Quaker upbringing, distressed by government warfare and treatment of blacks
> lectured all over country, but was harassed constantly

Source C: *Collier's Encyclopedia*
> brought up by Quaker family, received excellent education
> joined antislavery movement, Antislavery Society in New York
> tried to include voting rights for women in 14th Amendment, unsuccessful
> published periodicals, "The Revolution"
> arrested 1872 when she tried to vote in city election
> saw only four states accept women's voting right but paved way for 19th Amendment, women suffrage
> died 1906

Susan B. Anthony, who was born in Adams, Massachusetts in 1820, was an American feminist and reformer. Her Quaker upbringing encouraged independence and self-confidence and provided her with an excellent education. Susan was an eager student and learned to read and write at an early age. After her family moved to New York State, she left home to become a successful teacher and administrator at Canajoharie Academy.

While teaching, Susan began to take an active interest in the first of several public issues—the temperance movement. Later she joined the Antislavery Society in New York. In the early years, she was not allowed to speak in public. Not one to let the law or customs hold her back, Susan lectured widely throughout the country, even though she was constantly harassed by men in those efforts. After the Civil War, Susan fought for passage of the 14th Amendment to give voting rights to blacks. She tried unsuccessfully to include women in that amendment, and consequently was arrested for voting in an election near Rochester, New York.

The remainder of her life was dedicated to achieving social and political rights for women. Although she saw only four states accept women's voting rights before her death in 1906, Susan B. Anthony paved the way for the 19th Amendment giving women the right to vote.

RW 36

Compare/contrast.

Answers will vary. Sample:

There are several species and varieties of cats in the world, including 30 breeds of small domestic cats and many wild species. The domestic cat, spotted leopard, and African lion are three species that characterize those differences.

The domestic cat was one of the earliest household pets. Today there are more than 30 million in the United States alone. Even though they are the smallest of the cat family, they can still be wild and dangerous. In fact, farmers keep cats around their houses and barns to control the mice and rat populations. Larger and more dangerous is the spotted leopard, which is commonly found in East Asia. Known to be two to two-and-one-half feet long and weighing up to 30 pounds, this animal is grayish-brown in color and has many spots on its body. Sleeping days, the spotted leopard hunts birds and rodents at night for food. Contrasted with these two small cats is the king of beasts, the lion. Adult males can grow as large as 10 feet long and weigh up to 500 pounds. Found mostly in the open plains of Africa, this ferocious meat-eater will stalk and prey upon zebras and antelopes.

As you can see, there are many differences among members of the cat family. From the small domestic cat to the sizable lion, their physical features and habits vary widely.

RW 37

Cause/effect.

Answers will vary. Sample:

I recently attended a lecture given by Dr. Richard Cole entitled, "Running—The Total Exercise." He maintained there is a real need for Americans—both men and women—to exercise more often. Because most Americans devote so little time to any activity, they are unable to complete easy physical tests.

The physical and mental benefits of running were emphasized by Dr. Cole. First of all, running helps the body tolerate stress and strain, and also benefits skeletal muscles, the heart, and lungs. Likewise, running definitely increases a person's energy level. Not only will feelings of depression disappear, but it will also produce a more cheerful outlook on life. In addition, exercise reduces one's desire for food, tobacco, and alcohol.

Of the many different kinds of exercise, Dr. Cole presented a convincing argument for running. If Americans would just put on their jogging sneakers and run, they would soon notice the positive physical and mental changes.

RW 38

Compare/contrast.
Answers will vary. Sample:

Islam, Buddhism, and Hinduism are three of the world's greatest religions. Although they are not widely practiced in the United States, hundreds of millions of people belong to any one of the three.

Hinduism is one of the most popular, with more than 400 million followers. Most Hindus live in India. Since there is no single leader or person to follow, there are hundreds of gods common to every Indian household.

Buddhism started in India, but today is most popular in China, Japan, and Southeast Asia. Buddhism is the great oriental religion founded by Gautama Buddha. There are believed to be 550–600 million Buddhists who serve, respect, and idolize their god, Buddha.

In contrast, Islam is the religion for more than 500 million Arabs from Africa, Asia, and the Middle East. The followers of Islam, known as Mohammedans or Muslims, practice the teachings of Mohammed much as Christians follow the teachings of Christ. Muslims believe in just one god, Allah, and they study their bible, the Koran.

In conclusion, we should recognize that Hinduism, Buddhism, and Islam are three very popular religions. Although each is quite different from the other, together there are hundreds of millions of people who practice them.

RW 39

Sequence.
Answers will vary. Sample:

One of my favorite activities is planting and raising garden vegetables. Through experience I have learned the best way to produce a fine crop. Planning is the first step and that begins in February. I measure and plot the garden space, decide what vegetables to plant and then order seeds through a catalog company. When the seeds arrive, I read the packets to see the best planting time and mark it on a calendar. Before planting seeds, the soil must be prepared and the rows lined up. While planting, I am careful not to plant too shallow or too deep. Them I tamp down the soil gently and water. When the plants are young I cultivate around them to keep the weeds down. I also watch closely for pests that eat and kill the plants. Finally, I pick the ripe, delicious vegetables. If I have planned well and worked hard, the garden will definitely yield a fine crop of fresh produce.

RW 40

Compare/contrast.

Answers will vary. Sample:

Various kinds of oils are found in the world and the number of uses for them are truly amazing. There are more than ten different kinds of vegetable oils alone. Corn oil is used to make products like mayonnaise and salad dressing. While peanut oil is the second most widely eaten oil, soybean oil is the single most important used in the world today. On the other hand, most animal oils are not consumed. Lard, tallows, and greases, for example, are major products that come from hogs. One exception is butterfat products, like buttermilk, which we get from cows after the cream is separated from the raw milk. Likewise, marine, or water-type oils, are not usually eaten. The oil from whale's blubber can produce cosmetics and drugs. Other fish oils are used in paint products and lubricating greases. Of the many different oils available to us today, the vegetable, animal, and marine oils are three of the most common.

V

LETTER WRITING SKILLS AND ACTIVITIES

Probably the most practical and widely used form of writing is letter writing. This section covers several different types, including informal notes, friendly letters, and business letters. The business letters are divided into four categories, each with a separate purpose: a request, a complaint, a cover letter, and a problem that needs to be solved. Most business letters fall into one of these categories.

Letter writing may provide the best opportunity for emphasizing audience and purpose. When a live audience is involved, a letter is more likely than a report or a persuasive essay to elicit a response. Therefore, if they know a response is likely, students tend to express themselves more clearly and accurately. The purposes for letter writing are both practical and meaningful. At one time or another, most adults write some form of letter to express their feelings, communicate with family or friends, or deal with a particular problem. Students should have little trouble recognizing audience awareness and purposeful writing in this section. Subsequently, teachers can parallel the importance of these concepts to the other forms of writing.

A wide variety of letter forms is used and accepted, both in the schools and in the business world. Therefore, if the Business Letter Forms found on LW 24 and LW 25 are not consistent with what you are already using, feel free to substitute your own form. Whatever form serves your purposes, make sure that everyone uses the same one.

V. LETTER WRITING SKILLS AND ACTIVITIES

ORGANIZING FOR LETTER WRITING

Information: Like all forms of writing, letter writing requires some note taking and organizing prior to the actual rough draft. You must determine the following:

1. Who is the audience?

2. What is the purpose?

3. What do you want to say? What information is necessary to convey that message?

First, jot down your notes. Then organize those notes according to a plan. Finally, write those notes in sentences and paragraphs in a rough draft.

Directions: Read the situation and notes below.

Situation: You have been away from home as a camp counselor for two weeks. Write to your parents and tell them what you are doing and your reactions to the job.

   Audience: Your parents
   Purpose: Tell about job and reactions to it

Notes

Responsibilities—	8 campers in cabin. Help them to get along and to keep cabin clean. Teach beginning and advanced swimming classes all morning. Supervise recreation hall during free time. Help campers work on merit badges in afternoon.
Reactions and feelings—	Thoroughly enjoyable. Have common interests with many new people. Good campers, but have hard time getting along. Youngest one got homesick and left after first week.
At home—	How's family? Any friends call? Be home in two weeks.

Assignment: Write a letter home informing your parents about your work as a camp counselor. Develop three paragraphs using the notes outlined above.

AUDIENCE I

Directions: When you write a letter it makes a difference to whom you are writing. Read these two letters and answer the true/false statements that follow. Be prepared to support your answers.

Dear Mayor Hill:

It has come to my attention that a certain percentage of people living in the West Street area are refusing to cooperate with local regulations. Some are burning their trash and papers daily, even though pollution control laws were passed by the City Council last spring. Others are letting their pets wander throughout the neighborhood. Both these acts are violating local laws. Although there are other laws this group is ignoring, the two mentioned above are most disturbing to me. Your responsibility as the leader of this fine community is to assure that laws are enforced. I would appreciate your helping our neighborhood solve these problems. Thank you, Mayor Hill. I wish you well in the upcoming election.

Sincerely,
Harold Hoarsely

Dear Bruce:

Boy, are you lucky to have moved away from this city last year! Do you remember those three new families living at the other end of West Street? They have been burning their smelly trash every single day now. What they don't manage to burn remains in their yards for the rats and dogs. Speaking of dogs, Old Man Riggins must send his pack of mutts to my yard on purpose. You ought to see the old Johnson place! Those Adams kids have really destroyed it. You would never know those dummies at city hall ever wrote any of those laws dealing with pollution control and leash laws for pets. If Mayor Hill would get off the golf course and out of his swimming pool, he might be able to enforce the laws of this lousy town. He'll never get my vote next November because I'm moving!

Your friend,
Harold Hoarsely

---

1. These letters contain basically the same information. ————
2. There are more than two ways to express your feelings in a letter. ————
3. The letter to Bruce should have been written to the City Council to get better results. ————
4. Harold's letters will probably get a response from both people. ————
5. The letter to Mayor Hill should be changed to make it more convincing. ————

Assignment: You have been selected by your principal to tell the student council your feelings about the school cafeteria food and service. Write one letter to a friend and another to your student council expressing your feelings.

AUDIENCE II

Directions: Read the following audiences and situation.

1. a friend
2. your grandparents
3. the Better Business Bureau
4. a local newspaper

Situation: Your grandparents gave you $125 as a graduation present. You purchased a portable cassette tape recorder that could be used either in your car or at home. The recorder never worked properly, yet the local company, ACE Electronics, failed to fix it or replace it. The salesperson at ACE Electronics remembers selling the unit to you, but refuses to replace it because you do not have a copy of the warranty.

Assignment: Write a letter expressing your feelings to any *two* of the audiences listed above.

INFORMAL NOTE

Information: There are several occasions for writing an informal note. A thank-you, an invitation, or an apology are only a few examples. An informal note is generally written to someone you know quite well, and tends to be short in length and specific in purpose.

The informal note has five basic parts:

1. date

2. salutation

3. body

4. closing

5. signature

Of course the telephone has replaced note-writing in popularity; however, a written message can be very meaningful and lasting, especially when the purpose is to please someone.

Directions: Read the model below and notice its form and brief message.

October 14, 1982

Dear Joanne,

It's that time of year again! My annual Halloween party is all set for Saturday, October 30, 1982 at 7:30 p.m. at my house. The regular crew from school, as well as a few new friends from work, have all been invited. I'm sure we'll have a great time.

I don't have to remind you that costumes are required. We are still talking about your munchkin outfit at last year's affair. I can't wait to see your artistic and imaginative getup this year.

Write back soon with your acceptance. The party wouldn't be the same without you!

Yours truly,
Brenda

Assignment: Write an informal note to Brenda either accepting or declining her invitation to the Halloween party.

FRIENDLY LETTER

Information: Similar to informal notes, friendly letters are written to someone you know quite well. The purposes for writing are also varied, but the friendly letter might be more informative and lengthy. There could be several topics to express, especially if you have not seen the person for a while. The form of the friendly letter is also slightly different from an informal note. First, it includes a full heading with your return address and date. Second, the salutation and closing might be very informal and personal, and generally reflect the closeness of the friendship.

Directions: Read the model below and notice its form and style.

2427 Taylor Road
Heights, MT 59288
November 20, 1982

Hello Big Jim,

The other day as Phil and I attended the City League Football Championship, I decided it was time to write this long overdue letter.

Remember last year when St. Thomas Prep blasted East High 27–0 in that November blizzard? It didn't seem very cold when we were winning! Well, the tables turned this year. Even though the weather was seasonal, it was a cold day for the Saints from Thomas Prep. This year East had control the whole game and won 21–7. There's no doubt the team missed your speed and power at fullback.

Since you moved away last summer, there have been a few changes around here. Mr. Hixon, the new principal, seems to be friendly and concerned. He started an intramural sports program so that even uncoordinated klutzes like Phil and me can participate. Not only that, he has encouraged the Student Council and whole school to make suggestions for improvement in school activities. I think it will be a great year.

The neighborhood isn't quite the same since you left. The family that bought your house has three kids who are nothing but trouble. The oldest one was caught breaking windows in the Canterbury School last week. The parents don't seem to care where they are or what they do. Oh, well, we'll survive!

Write back soon and let us know what's happening.

The Taylor Road Flash,
Richie Levine

Assignment: Write a friendly letter to someone you know whom you have not seen in some time. Follow the form and style of the model shown above. Be sure to mail the letter!

BUSINESS LETTER: FORM

Information: There are two basic forms for business letters: *block form* and *modified block form*. In the block form, the heading, inside address, salutation, body, closing, and signature begin at the left margin of the paper. In the modified block form, the heading, closing, and signature begin at the right of center and do not extend beyond the right margin. The first word in each paragraph in the modified block form is indented. Always use plain white paper for business letters whether you hand-write or type them. Be sure to make your letters brief and to the point.

Directions: Read the two models below. On the line above each one, write whether the model is in block form or in modified block form.

Model 1 _____

                                     2781 Marathon Road
                                     Rochester, MA 01989
                                     November 1, 1982

Station Manager
WBZ Radio
Livingston, MA 01997

Dear Station Manager:

_____

_____

_____

_____

                                     Sincerely,
                                     Bill Nee

Model 2 _____

2781 Marathon Road
Rochester, MA 01989
November 1, 1982

Station Manager
WBZ Radio
Livingston, MA 01997

Dear Station Manager:

_____

_____

_____

_____

Sincerely,
Bill Nee

Assignment: Using one of the model forms shown above, write a letter to the station manager requesting a copy of the October 30, 1982 political editorial entitled, "The Middle East: Beginning and End of Civilization." You plan to enclose 75 cents for postage and handling.

LW 6

BUSINESS LETTER: REQUEST I

Information: One purpose for writing letters is to request something from your audience. You might want to order a catalog, buy tickets to a concert, or receive more information about an advertised product. Whatever the purpose, you must remember to use proper form, proofread for any mechanical errors, and give your audience all the information they need to respond to your request.

Directions: Read the model request letter below and answer the questions that follow.

> 472 High Avenue
> Columbia, GA 31700
>
> Columbia Modular Homes
> 1119 East Avenue
> Columbia, GA 31700
>
> Dear Sir or Madam:
>
> I noticed your modular home brochure at the Home and Garden Show last weekend at the Civic Center. There was not much specific information in those brochures. Therefore, I would like you to either mail me more detailed construction specifications or notify one of your representatives to contact me in person.
>
> Sincerely,
> Edward Steitler

1. Who is the audience? _____

2. What is the purpose for writing? _____

_____

_____

3. Has the writer given all the information necessary for the audience to respond? If not, what else is needed?

_____

_____

4. Has this person used acceptable business letter form? _____

5. Are there any mechanical errors? _____ If so, what are they?

_____

_____

_____

BUSINESS LETTER: REQUEST II

Directions: Read the situation and complete the assignment below.

Situation: You saw the following advertisement in a magazine. You want to see their catalog so that you can order some tapes and records.

BUYING TAPES AND RECORD ALBUMS?

discount prices—25% savings

We have all your favorite rock or
country stars' recordings!
Send for our free catalog

YOU WON'T BELIEVE OUR PRICES!

Acme Sound Shop   11802 Hooper Avenue
Bridgeton, Texas 75588

Assignment: Write a business letter to the Acme Sound Shop. When writing this letter, be sure to:

1. Use an acceptable business letter form.

2. Give complete and accurate information so that the store can respond.

3. Proofread for any mechanical errors.

BUSINESS LETTER: PROBLEM AND SOLUTION I

Information: Occasionally a problem develops and you must attempt to solve that problem by writing a business letter to the audience. Perhaps you have ordered a product that arrived damaged or requested some information that you never received. In any case, you must fully explain the situation and explain what the audience should do to solve the problem. Make sure you are polite when writing; the problem may only be an honest error.

Directions: Read the model below and answer the questions that follow.

May 7, 1983

12 Church Street
Ogden, MN

Manager
Newbury Springs Campground
Newbury, WV

Dear Manager:

On April 5, 1983, I sent you a letter requesting campsite reservations for August 15–17. I also enclosed a check for $20 to reserve a camper site. Did you get them? To date, I have not received confirmation of those reservations. Since my vacation is tightly scheduled, I hope you will respond as quickly as possible. If I don't hear from you within ten days, I will be forced to make alternative plans.

Sincerely,
Bernice Cobbett

---

1. Who is the audience? _____

2. What is the problem? _____

_____

3. What is the writer's solution? _____

_____

4. Has all the necessary information been given in the letter? _____ If not, what else is needed? _____

_____

_____

5. List any problems with form or mechanics. _____

_____

_____

BUSINESS LETTER: PROBLEM AND SOLUTION II

Directions: Read the situation.

Situation: Your school drama club ordered 25 T-shirts with the words "See you in Camelot" printed on each. These shirts will be worn by club members to advertise an upcoming play. You mailed the Orleans Outlet Store a check for $123.75 ($4.95 per shirt) to cover the order. However, only 15 shirts were received. As president of the club, you want to write to the company at Route 488, Orleans, New York 13700.

Assignment: Write a business letter to the Orleans Outlet Store to solve the problem. When writing this letter, be sure to:

1. Use acceptable business letter form.

2. Give complete and accurate information.

3. Solve the problem.

4. Proofread for mechanical errors.

BUSINESS LETTER: COMPLAINT I

Information: This type of business letter is used after you have made every attempt to solve the problem. Like the problem/solution letter, the tone of your letter should be polite. However, your solution is more forceful and direct.

Your audience most likely has been "To whom it may concern" or "Sir or Madam." The complaint letter should now be directed to someone in charge, perhaps the Manager or the President. Remember, your primary purpose is still to solve the problem. Therefore, it is important to carefully explain the situation forcefully and politely.

Directions: Read the model complaint letter below and answer the questions that follow.

---

21 Green Street
Graham, NH 03599
September 27, 1982

Mayor Edwin Riley
Municipal Building
Centerville, NH 03928

Dear Mayor Riley:

I have tried, without success, on three occasions to correct an obvious error of mistaken identity. On June 12, 1982 I received a bill in the amount of $10 for a parking violation in your city on May 30, 1982. I attempted to explain, first by telephone and later in two letters, to the Police Department that I was not in Centerville on that date. In fact, I was in Boston visiting relatives over the Memorial Day holiday. Yesterday, I received another bill for $10 plus a $5 late fee. An attached letter threatened to notify the Department of Motor Vehicles of the delinquency so that I could not renew my license.

I resent this whole situation! What additional action do I have to take to resolve this error? I have contacted my lawyer and will request a lawsuit if _you_ do not do something immediately. It is apparent your Police Department cannot handle it.

Respectfully,
John W. Smith

---

1. Has Mr. Smith attempted to solve the problem? _____

2. Is the information clearly stated? _____ If not, what else is needed?

_____

3. How does Mr. Smith still attempt to solve the problem? _____

_____

4. How might you have written this complaint differently? _____

_____

BUSINESS LETTER: COMPLAINT II

Directions: Read the situation.

Situation: The Treadwell Tire Company on Park Avenue in Milton, Arkansas sold you four new radial tires that were guaranted for 40,000 miles. One of the front tires blew out five months after your purchase. As a result of the blowout, you lost control of the car, hit a pothole, and broke the left front shock and spring. You want the tire, shock, and spring replaced free of charge since the tire was defective. The local manager refused to cooperate. He said you cannot prove the tire was defective.

Assignment: Write to the President of Treadwell Tire Company in Fair Ridge, Ohio 45289 concerning this situation. Be sure to:

1. Explain the situation completely and accurately.

2. Complain politely and offer your solution.

3. Use acceptable business letter form.

4. Proofread for mechanical errors.

BUSINESS LETTER: COVER LETTER I

Information: When you apply for a job or when you are sending important information to someone, a cover letter should be attached to the application or the information. Use an acceptable business letter form and give the audience a brief summary of why you are writing and what you have attached. If the cover letter accompanies a job application or résumé, be sure to highlight your strengths and specific skills.

Directions: Read the model cover letter below and answer the questions that follow.

28 South Street
Danbury, SC 29598
January 18, 1983

Personnel Manager
Smithson, Inc.
Route 7
Ventnor, SC 29391

Dear Personnel Manager:

I noticed with interest your advertisement for an assistant welder in last Sunday's paper. I have attached a résumé for your information, hoping you will send me an application. I am available for an interview any time.

Please note that I recently graduated from Middle Valley Vocational and Technical School, where I successfully completed two years of welding classes. I have also worked for Wilkerson Welding for the past two years.

I look forward to hearing from you. You may call me at home at 442-8968.

Sincerely,
Wilfred Williams

1. Does the cover letter explain why Wilfred Williams is writing? _____

2. What two things does the writer want as a result of his writing this letter?

_____

_____

_____

3. Does the writer list any specific skills he has learned? _____
   Should he? _____ Why or why not? _____

_____

4. Is there any other information he should have included in the cover letter? _____ If so, what? _____

_____

5. Would you, as personnel manager, grant the writer an interview? Why or why not? _____

_____

BUSINESS LETTER: COVER LETTER II

Directions: Read the situation.

Situation: The following advertisement appeared in your local paper's Sunday edition. You want to receive an application and be given an interview. You plan to attach a résumé with your request. (For the purposes of this assignment, make up any information necessary to complete the letter and résumé.)

> Assistant Manager Trainee. Ambitious person with pleasant personality needed. Restaurant experience helpful but not necessary. Apply to Manager, Red Rooster Restaurants, 1204 Monroe Avenue, Albany, Alabama 35373.

Assignment: Write a cover letter to the manager. When writing this letter, be sure to:

1. Use acceptable business letter form.

2. Explain why you are writing.

3. Highlight your interests, experiences, and background.

4. Proofread for any mechanical errors.

REVISING I: FORM AND MECHANICS

Information: There are several forms of letter writing, and the one you use depends upon the type of letter and its purpose. Whether you are writing an informal note, a friendly letter, or a business letter, make sure the form suits the purpose.

The mechanics of a letter, such as spelling, punctuation, capitalization, and grammar, must be accurate. Otherwise, your intended audience will be distracted and the message may lose its importance.

Directions: Read the situation and letter below and underline any problems in form or mechanics.

Situation: A letter has been written to the principal of an elementary school in hopes of getting a job as a teacher's aide in the summer school program.

Howard Forbs, Principal
Kennedy elementary school
Homesdale CA, 95332

Dear Mr. Forbs,

I have recently completed High School and will be entering Hillside community college in in September. I understand there are several opening in the Kennedy school for teachers aides this summer. I would like to be considered. For this position because I enjoy working with kids and I may even want to teach someday.

I have worked with kids at the lakemont community center and at a day camp. I hope you will consider me for the job.

Sincerely
Frank Lisi

Assignment: Identify the problems with form and mechanics in this letter. Then rewrite the letter after revising the mistakes.

REVISING II: MESSAGE

Information: Form and mechanics are certainly important aspects of all letter writing. But if the message is not clearly understood by your audience, they will not likely respond as you intend. There are two things you can do to make your message clear. First, organize your ideas by topic *before* writing the rough draft. Second, let a friend, classmate, or family member read the rough draft.

Directions: Read the situation and model letter below. Then answer the questions that follow.

Situation: You went to a restaurant recently with two out-of-state friends who were visiting for a few days. You had to wait an unreasonable amount of time to be served, the meal was cold, and the waiter was rude. The delay caused you to be late to a concert and you were thoroughly embarrassed. Express your feelings to the manager.

21990 Center Road
Solitude, VT 05203
September 15, 1982

Manager
Dressler's Restaurant
Solitude, VT 05203

Dear Manager:

   Two out-of-state friends were visiting me last week and I wanted to treat them to a special dinner at Dressler's Restaurant. I heard from several people that Dressler's food and service are the best in the area. After my experience, I would never recommend your establishment to anybody! My friends are from New Orleans, a city with great restaurants, and I wanted to show off Northern cooking. Boy was I embarrassed.
   I don't know who is at fault, but I would urge you to take a close look at the whole operation at Dressler's. If you don't correct these problems, you won't be in business much longer.

                              Sincerely,
                              Madge Harper

---

1. Does the manager know how the writer feels? _____

2. Does the writer specifically state what the problems are? _____

   What has she failed to say? _____

   _____

3. How would you, as manager, react or respond to this letter? _____

   _____

Assignment: Rewrite this letter, clearly and specifically expressing your message to the manager.

PRACTICE AND REVIEW I

Directions: Read the situation and determine the audience, purpose, and type of letter (informal, friendly, business) to write.

Situation: Your wealthy uncle is a businessman who lives in London, England. He mailed you the perfect birthday gift. (The gift is whatever you want it to be.) Although it arrived late and the package was slightly damaged, your gift was not harmed. His address is: 4 Garden Estates, London.

Audience: _____

Purpose: _____

Type of letter: _____

Assignment: Write to your uncle to thank him for his generosity and thoughtfulness. When writing this letter, be sure to:

1. Use an acceptable form.

2. Make your message clear.

3. Revise any mechanical errors in spelling, capitalization, punctuation, sentence structure, etc.

PRACTICE AND REVIEW II

Directions: Read the situation and determine the audience, purpose, and type of letter (informal, friendly, business) to write.

Situation: You recently read a book, *The Challengers,* by Diane Pettibone Fox. Because it was the best historical novel you have ever read, you decided to inquire about three other novels she wrote. The local librarian gave you the address of the publishing company: Coronet Publishers, Inc., 205 Sylvia Avenue, Western City, Florida 31621.

Audience: _____

Purpose: _____

Type of letter: _____

Assignment: Write to the publishing company to ask for information and an order form so that you can purchase the author's other three novels. When writing this letter, be sure to:

1. Use an acceptable form.

2. Make your message clear.

3. Revise any mechanical errors in spelling, capitalization, punctuation, sentence structure, etc.

PRACTICE AND REVIEW III

Directions: Read the situation and determine the audience, purpose, and type of letter (informal, friendly, business) to write.

Situation: A classified ad for an office secretary told you to apply in person to Henderson Electronics, Old State Road, Clifton, Kentucky 41508. Because there were so many applicants, the Assistant Personnel Manager, Mrs. Eleanor Howell, gave everyone an application. She asked you to return it with a cover letter within five days.

Audience: _____

Purpose: _____

Type of letter: _____

Assignment: Write a cover letter to be sent along with your application. When writing this letter, be sure to:

1. Use an acceptable form.

2. Make your message clear.

3. Revise any mechanical errors in spelling, capitalization, punctuation, sentence structure, etc.

PRACTICE AND REVIEW IV

Directions: Read the situation and determine the audience, purpose, and type of letter (informal, friendly, business) to write.

Situation: You signed an agreement with R.V.A. Record Club (P.O. Box 9701, New York, New York 10200) to buy eight records or tapes at $7.95 each within one year. The contract stated that you did *not* have to accept their monthly selections; it was possible to buy from the catalog at any time. However, R.V.A. has been billing you $7.95 plus $.75 postage and handling for the past three months. As yet, you have not selected any records or tapes.

Audience: _____

Purpose: _____

Type of letter: _____

Assignment: Write to the record club to solve the problem. When writing this letter, be sure to:

1. Use an acceptable form.

2. Make your message clear.

3. Revise any mechanical errors in spelling, capitalization, punctuation, sentence structure, etc.

PRACTICE AND REVIEW V

Directions: Read the situation and determine the audience, purpose, and type of letter (informal, friendly, business) to write.

Situation: You live in Mountainside Apartments complex owned by J.L. Rentals, Inc., of Bingham, Colorado 80608. The superintendent of that complex has been careless in his duties and rude in dealing with the tenants. Among other things, he has failed to repair plumbing and electrical problems, has neglected to keep the grounds attractive and litter-free, and has used profanity repeatedly in dealing with renters.

Audience: _____

Purpose: _____

Type of letter: _____

Assignment: Write to the owners to inform them of this situation. When writing this letter, be sure to:

1. Use an acceptable form.

2. Make your message clear.

3. Revise any mechanical errors in spelling, capitalization, punctuation, sentence structure, etc.

PRACTICE AND REVIEW VI

Directions: Read the situation and determine the audience, purpose, and type of letter (informal, friendly, business) to write.

Situation: Your closest friend went to a college that is more than 1,200 miles from home. Therefore, you have not seen him or her since early September and will not likely get together until Christmas vacation.

Audience: ————————————————————————

Purpose: ————————————————————————

Type of letter: ————————————————————

Assignment: Write a letter to your friend bringing him or her up to date on all the latest school, family, and social news. When writing this letter, be sure to:

1. Use an acceptable form.

2. Make your message clear.

3. Revise any mechanical errors in spelling, capitalization, punctuation, sentence structure, etc.

LETTER WRITING: OUTLINE FORM OF INFORMAL AND FRIENDLY LETTERS

Heading
(Informal—date only)

Salutation

Body

Closing

Signature

LETTER WRITING: OUTLINE FORM OF BUSINESS LETTER (BLOCK FORM)

Heading

Inside address

Salutation

Body

Closing

Signature

LETTER WRITING: OUTLINE FORM OF BUSINESS LETTER (MODIFIED BLOCK FORM)

Heading

Inside address

Salutation

Body

Closing

Signature

LETTER WRITING TOPICS

Write a letter to: a friend
a family member
your congressman
your principal
your mayor
a local merchant
the police department
a local museum
the newspaper

About: a trip you took
a graduation gift sent to you
a new proposed law
a way to improve the school
the need for a traffic light at a
    dangerous intersection
a poor product
heroic actions while apprehending
    a robber
information you need for a history
    project
the comments of a politician

ANSWER KEY

LW 1

Answers will vary. Sample:

Dear Folks,

After two weeks at camp, I must say I'm having a thoroughly enjoyable time. Most of the counselors here are very friendly and I have quite a bit in common with two of them. The campers are well-behaved, although the youngest one went home after the first week because of homesickness.

There are now eight campers in my cabin and my job is to help them get along with each other and keep the cabin in order. In the morning, I teach beginning and advanced swimming classes and I work with the older ones on their merit badge requirements after lunch. During free time I supervise the recreation hall. You can imagine I am rather busy every day with these responsibilities.

How's everything at home? Have any of my friends called? I'll be home in two weeks and look forward to relaxing for the rest of the summer.

Love,
Jeannie

LW 2

1. True.
2. True.
3. False.
4. True or False depending on reasoning.
5. False.

Assignment: Answers will vary. The two letters should contain the same information, but should be different in style. The two examples should provide a model for students' writings.

LW 3

Dear Bill:

Do you remember the cassette tape recorder my grandparents gave me for graduation? Even though it cost $125 and looked fantastic, that piece of junk never really worked properly. About a week after I got it, I took it back to ACE Electronics for repair or replacement. However, just because the warranty was lost, they refused to do either. I lost my temper, yelled at the manager, and left in a huff, promising to create a problem.

Well, those people will pay for treating customers that way! I have just written *The Times'* "help" column, the Better Business Bureau, and the local television station. I hope their business really suffers for the way they treated me! Make sure you tell everyone not to do business with ACE Electronics—ever.

Your friend,
Paul

Better Business Bureau:
I feel obligated to inform you of a problem I had with ACE Electronics (in my town). My grandparents bought me a cassette tape recorder for $125 from that company just two weeks ago and gave it to me last week for a graduation present. The recorder never worked properly. Although I returned it to their shop with the sales slip, they refused to replace or repair it. The manager insisted I provide the warranty, which was lost somehow. He admitted the recorder was defective and was purchased only two weeks ago, yet he still refused to help me.

I don't think ACE Electronics acted in a proper businesslike manner. Please help me with my problem.

Sincerely,
Paul Hammond

LW 4

Answers will vary. Sample:

October 19, 1982

Dear Brenda,
You can count on me to attend your annual Halloween party on Saturday, October 30, 1982. I wouldn't miss it for any reason! You always manage to organize everything so well, and your display of food would impress a New York chef.

I have designed another costume and can't wait to show it off. But I'm sure yours will be just as impressive.

I'm looking forward to a great time.

Your friend,
Joanne

LW 5

Answers will vary. Students should attempt to develop several topics within the letter in an informal manner. The example should provide a model for students' writings.

LW 6

Model 1: Modified Block Form.
Model 2: Block Form.
Assignment: Answers will vary. Sample:

2781 Marathon Road
Rochester, MA 01989
November 1, 1982

Station Manager
WBZ Radio
Livingston, MA 01997

Dear Station Manager:

I listened to your political editorial entitled, "The Middle East: Beginning and End of Civilization," on October 30, 1982. I am writing a research paper on this topic and would appreciate your sending me a written copy of that editorial.

I have enclosed 75 cents for postage and handling, so that you can send a copy to me at the above address.

Sincerely,
Bill Nee

LW 7

1. Columbia Modular Homes.
2. To get more information, such as construction specifications, on this company's modular homes.
3. Yes.
4. Yes.
5. Yes, the letter is not dated.

LW 8

Answers will vary. Sample:

1210 Smith Drive
Bridgeton, Texas 75588
April 5, 1983

Acme Sound Shop
11802 Hooper Avenue
Bridgeton, Texas 75588

Dear Sir or Madam:

I saw your advertisement for discount prices on tapes and record albums. I would appreciate your sending me the free catalog and price list as soon as possible to the above address.

I am quite interested in buying some tapes if the selections and prices are satisfactory.

Sincerely,
George Harmon

LW 9

1. The manager of the campground.
2. Reservations have not been confirmed.
3. Either contact her within ten days or she will cancel the reservations.
4. Yes.
5. Zip codes should be used, and date should be underneath the return address.

LW 10

Answers will vary. Sample:

17 Lakeview Circle
Rochester, MA 01989
January 11, 1983

Orleans Outlet Store
Route 488
Orleans, NY 13700

Dear Sir or Madam:

Our drama club recently ordered 25 T-shirts with the words "See you in Camelot" written on them to advertise our upcoming play. As president, I sent you a check for $123.75 ($4.95 per shirt) to cover the cost of the T-shirts. Unfortunately, we only received 15 of the 25 ordered.

Is there another package en route? If not, would you please send the remaining 10 T-shirts as soon as possible? Our play will be performed soon and all of us want to wear these shirts before the play.

Sincerely,
Ben Murray

LW 11

1. Yes.
2. Yes.

3. He has contacted his lawyer and threatened a lawsuit.
4. Might have written the last sentence a bit more politely.

LW 12

Answers will vary. Sample:

> 33 Gordon Street
> Milton, Arkansas 73900
> May 3, 1983

President
Treadwell Tire Company
Fair Ridge, Ohio 45289

Dear Mr. President:

About five months ago, the Treadwell Tire Company on Park Avenue in Milton, Arkansas sold me four new radial tires that were guaranteed for 40,000 miles. Last week on the way home from work, the right front tire blew. Consequently, I lost control of the car, hit a pothole, and broke the right front shock and spring.

Since the tire blowout was the cause of this accident and since the tires were guaranteed, I went to the store manager in Milton for replacement of the tire, shock, and spring. He refused to replace anything, insisting that there was no way to prove the tire was at fault.

Perhaps no one can <u>prove</u> fault, but I still feel your company is responsible for guaranteeing those tires and any resulting damage. I hope you accept this responsibility. If not, I'll be inclined to take my business elsewhere in the future.

> Sincerely,
> Diane Stephano

LW 13

1. Yes.
2. He wants an application and an interview.
3. Yes. Yes. So this company knows he has the background and experience to fill the job's responsibilities.
4. No.
5. Yes. He wrote the letter well and identified education and experience. He seems to be qualified for the position.

LW 14

Answers will vary. Sample:

331 Pine Street
Albany, AL 35373
February 11, 1983

Manager
Red Rooster Restaurant
1204 Monroe Avenue
Albany, AL 35373

Dear Manager:

I noticed your advertisement in last Sunday's paper for an Assistant Manager Trainee. I am sending you my résumé hoping you will return an application for the position. Although I do not have any restaurant experience, I enjoy working with people, have worked very hard at previous jobs and look forward to a career in the restaurant business.

I look forward to hearing from you and completing the application.

Sincerely,
Greg Washington

LW 15

Answers will vary. Sample:

5 Washburn Street
Homesdale, CA 95332
555-1212
June 17, 1983

Mr. Howard Forbs, Principal
Kennedy Elementary School
Homesdale, CA 95332

Dear Mr. Forbs:

I have recently completed high school and will be entering Hillside Community College in September. I understand there are several openings in the Kennedy School for teachers' aides this summer. I would like to be considered for this position because I enjoy working with kids. I may even want to teach someday.

I have worked with elementary-aged children at the Lakemont Community Center and at the Homesdale Day Camp. I hope you will consider me for the job by writing to the above address. For your convenience I have included my telephone number. I will be available for an interview at any time.

Sincerely,
Frank Lisi

LW 16

1. Yes.
2. No. She never stated specifically that the food was cold, the waiter was rude, and that the delay was unreasonable.
3. I may not respond. If I responded, I would ask what the specific problems were and possibly invite her to a free meal.

Assignment: Answers will vary. Sample:

> 21990 Center Road
> Solitude, VT 05203
> September 15, 1982

Manager
Dressler's Restaurant
Solitude, VT 05203

Dear Manager:

Two out-of-state friends were visiting me last week and I wanted to treat them to a special dinner at Dressler's Restaurant. I heard from several people that Dressler's food and service were the best in the area. My friends came from New Orleans, a city with great restaurants, and I wanted to show off Northern cooking.

After my experience, however, I would not be able to recommend your establishment to anyone. First of all, a rude and disinterested waiter ignored us for nearly 30 minutes before taking our order. Then we waited 45 additional minutes for our meal. Everything was cold and soggy. As a result of this experience, I was thoroughly embarrassed and we were late for a concert.

I don't know who is at fault—the waiter, the chefs or the manager. But I would urge you to take a closer look at the whole operation at Dressler's. If you don't correct these problems, you won't be in business much longer.

> Sincerely,
> Madge Harper

LW 17

Audience: Your wealthy uncle.
Purpose: To thank him for the gift.
Type of letter: Informal.
Assignment: Answers will vary. Sample:

> October 12, 1982

Dear Uncle Phil,

Your ability to find the perfect gift has always amazed me! The bone-white cardigan sweater you sent for my birthday is absolutely beautiful and it fits like it was especially made for me. How did you know I wanted a cardigan this year? You're really terrific.

Although the damaged package arrived two days late and looked like it swam the Atlantic, the sweater itself was unharmed and the two-day delay was well worth it.

Thanks again, Uncle Phil, for your thoughtfulness and generosity. I shall think of you every time I wear it.

Your loving niece,
Melissa

LW 18

Audience: Coronet Publishers, Inc.
Purpose: To request how to obtain other books.
Type of letter: Business letter of request.
Assignment: Answers will vary. Sample:

115 Gracie Avenue
New York, NY 11001
March 3, 1983

Coronet Publishers, Inc.
205 Sylvia Avenue
Western City, FL 31621

Dear Sir or Madam:

I recently read *The Challengers* by Diane Pettibone Fox and can honestly say it was the best historical novel I've ever read. I understand Ms. Fox has written three other novels, yet I've not been able to locate them in my library or local book stores. Are they still in print? Can they be purchased through you? I would appreciate your helping me locate these books, as I look forward to reading them. If you have this information, please contact me as soon as possible at the above address.

Sincerely,
Catherine Lyndon

LW 19

Audience: Mrs. Eleanor Howell.
Purpose: To return the application with a cover letter.
Type of letter: Business letter with a cover letter.
Assignment: Answers will vary. Sample:

224 St. Paul Avenue
Clifton, Kentucky 41508
555-1212
April 10, 1983

Mrs. Eleanor Howell
Assistant Personnel Manager
Henderson Electronics
Old State Road
Clifton, Kentucky 41508

Dear Mrs. Howell:

I thank you very much for giving me an application for the position of office secretary at Henderson Electronics. I have completed the attached application, hoping that my secretarial skills and experiences will permit you to grant me an interview.

I know several people who have worked or are presently working at Henderson. They all have spoken so positively about the attitude and opportunities there. Obviously, I look forward to hearing from you and hope you will consider me for an interview.

Sincerely,
Kelly McGuire

LW 20

Audience: R.V.A. Record Club.
Purpose: To complain about billing procedures.
Type of letter: Business letter of complaint.
Assignment: Answers will vary. Sample:

918 Circle Lane
Winston, NJ 07001
August 7, 1982

R.V.A. Record Club
P.O. Box 9701
New York, NY 10200

To whom it may concern:

About four months ago I joined the R.V.A. Record Club and agreed to buy eight records or tapes at $7.95 each within one year. I was not required, according to the contract, to accept your monthly selections. To date, I have not made any selections. However, you have billed me $7.95 plus $.75 postage and handling for the past three months. These billings violate the contract, especially since I haven't ordered or received any tapes or records yet.

I refuse to pay for something not received or ordered. Please solve this problem by crediting me $26.10. Otherwise, I shall be forced to drop my membership from the club and possibly see my lawyer for assistance.

Sincerely,
Keith Mathers

LW 21

Audience: J. L. Rentals, Inc.
Purpose: To complain about the superintendent.
Type of letter: Business letter of complaint.
Assignment: Answers will vary. Sample:

15-A Westside Lane
Bingham, CO 80608
January 11, 1983

J. L. Rentals, Inc.
Bingham, CO 80608

Dear Sir or Madam:

I wish to alert you to a problem at the Mountainside Apartment Complex that has bothered me and several other tenants for the past few months. Your superintendent, Mr. Louis Vanders, has been neglectful in his duties and rude to the tenants. Among other things, he has failed to repair plumbing and electrical problems, has neglected to keep the grounds attractive and litter-free, and has used profanity constantly when dealing with renters here.

Several of us are considering breaking our leases and moving elsewhere unless something is done about this problem. Mr. Vanders should either change his attitude or you should seriously consider hiring another superintendent. I suggest you do one or the other, or else more serious problems may develop.

Sincerely,
Gary Beamish

LW 22

Audience: Your close friend.
Purpose: To inform your friend of activities at home.
Type of letter: Friendly.
Assignment: Answers will vary. Sample: